THE WRITINGS IN PROSE AND VERSE OF

RUDYARD KIPLING

THE FIVE NATIONS

NEW YORK
CHARLES SCRIBNER'S SONS
1917

DEDICATION

Before a midnight breaks in storm,
　Or herded sea in wrath,
Ye know what wavering gusts inform
　The greater tempest's path;
　　Till the loosed wind
　　Drive all from mind,
Except Distress, which, so will prophets cry,
O'ercame them, houseless, from the unhinting sky.

Ere rivers league against the land
　In piratry of flood,
Ye know what waters slip and stand
　Where seldom water stood.
　　Yet who will note,
　　Till fields afloat,
And washen carcass and the returning well,
Trumpet what these poor heralds strove to tell?

v

Ye know who use the Crystal Ball
(To peer by stealth on Doom),
The Shade that, shaping first of all,
Prepares an empty room.
Then doth It pass
Like breath from glass,
But, on the extorted vision bowed intent,
No man considers why It came or went.

Before the years reborn behold
Themselves with stranger eye,
And the sport-making Gods of old,
Like Samson slaying, die,
Many shall hear
The all-pregnant sphere
Bow to the birth and sweat, but—speech denied—
Sit dumb or—dealt in part—fall weak and wide.

Yet instant to fore-shadowed need
The eternal balance swings;
That winged men the Fates may breed
So soon as Fate hath wings.
These shall possess
Our littleness,
And in the imperial task (as worthy) lay
Up our lives' all to piece one giant day.

vi

CONTENTS

LIST OF ILLUSTRATIONS

THE SEA AND THE HILLS

Who hath desired the Sea?—the sight of salt water
　unbounded—
The heave and the halt and the hurl and the crash of
　the comber wind-hounded?
The sleek-barrelled swell before storm, grey, foam-
　less, enormous, and growing—
Stark calm on the lap of the Line or the crazy-eyed
　hurricane blowing—
His Sea is no showing the same—his Sea and the
　same 'neath each showing—
　　　His Sea as she slackens or thrills?
So and no otherwise—so and no otherwise hillmen
　desire their Hills!

Who hath desired the Sea?—the immense and con-
　temptuous surges?
The shudder, the stumble, the swerve, as the star-
　stabbing bowsprit emerges?

3

THE SEA AND THE HILLS

The orderly clouds of the Trades, and the ridged,
  roaring sapphire thereunder—
Unheralded cliff-haunting flaws and the head-sail's
  low-volleying thunder—
His Sea in no wonder the same—his Sea and the same
  through each wonder:
          His Sea as she rages or stills?
So and no otherwise—so and no otherwise hillmen
  desire their Hills.

Who hath desired the Sea?   Her menaces swift as
  her mercies,
The in-rolling walls of the fog and the silver-winged
  breeze that disperses?
The unstable mined berg going South and the calvings
  and groans that declare it;
White water half-guessed overside and the moon
  breaking timely to bare it;
His Sea as his fathers have dared—his Sea as his
  children shall dare it—
          His Sea as she serves him or kills?
So and no otherwise—so and no otherwise hillmen
  desire their Hills.

Who hath desired the Sea? Her excellent loneliness
  rather
Than forecourts of kings, and her outermost pits than
  the streets where men gather

4

THE SEA AND THE HILLS

Inland, among dust, under trees—inland where the
    slayer may slay him
Inland, out of reach of her arms, and the bosom
    whereon he must lay him—
His Sea at the first that betrayed—at the last that
    shall never betray him—
        His Sea that his being fulfils ?
So and no otherwise—so and no otherwise hillmen
    desire their Hills.

THE BELL BUOY

THEY christened my brother of old—
  And a saintly name he bears—
They gave him his place to hold
  At the head of the belfry-stairs,
  Where the minster-towers stand
And the breeding kestrels cry.
  Would I change with my brother a league inland?
(Shoal! 'Ware shoal!) Not I!

In the flush of the hot June prime,
  O'er smooth flood-tides afire,
I hear him hurry the chime
  To the bidding of checked Desire;
  Till the sweated ringers tire
And the wild bob-majors die.
  Could I wait for my turn in the godly choir?
(Shoal! 'Ware shoal!) Not I!

THE BELL BUOY

When the smoking scud is blown,
  When the greasy wind-rack lowers,
Apart and at peace and alone,
  He counts the changeless hours.
  He wars with darkling Powers
(I war with a darkling sea);
  Would he stoop to my work in the gusty mirk?
(Shoal! 'Ware shoal!) Not he!

There was never a priest to pray,
  There was never a hand to toll,
When they made me guard of the bay,
  And moored me over the shoal.
  I rock, I reel, and I roll—
My four great hammers ply—
  Could I speak or be still at the Church's will?
(Shoal! 'Ware shoal!) Not I!

The landward marks have failed,
  The fog-bank glides unguessed,
The seaward lights are veiled,
  The spent deep feigns her rest:
  But my ear is laid to her breast,
I lift to the swell—I cry!
  Could I wait in sloth on the Church's oath?
(Shoal! 'Ware shoal!) Not I!

7

THE BELL BUOY

At the careless end of night
  I thrill to the nearing screw,
I turn in the nearing light
  And I call to the drowsy crew;
  And the mud boils foul and blue
As the blind bow backs away.
  Will they give me their thanks if they clear the
    banks?
(Shoal! 'Ware shoal!) Not they!

The beach-pools cake and skim,
  The bursting spray-heads freeze,
I gather on crown and rim
  The grey, grained ice of the seas,
  Where, sheathed from bitt to trees,
The plunging colliers lie.
  Would I barter my place for the Church's grace?
(Shoal! 'Ware shoal!) Not I!

Through the blur of the whirling snow,
  Or the black of the inky sleet,
The lanterns gather and grow,
  And I look for the homeward fleet.
  Rattle of block and sheet—
" Ready about—stand by!"
  Shall I ask them a fee ere they fetch the quay?
(Shoal! 'Ware shoal!) Not I!

THE BELL BUOY

I dip and I surge and I swing
 In the rip of the racing tide,
By the gates of doom I sing,
 On the horns of death I ride.
 A ship-length overside,
Between the course and the sand,
 Fretted and bound I bide
  Peril whereof I cry.
 Would I change with my brother a league inland?
(*Shoal! 'Ware shoal!*) Not I!

CRUISERS

As our mother the Frigate, bepainted and fine,
Made play for her bully the Ship of the Line;
So we, her bold daughters by iron and fire,
Accost and decoy to our masters' desire.

Now pray you consider what toils we endure,
Night-walking wet sea-lanes, a guard and a lure;
Since half of our trade is that same pretty sort
As mettlesome wenches do practise in port.

For this is our office: to spy and make room,
As hiding yet guiding the foe to their doom;
Surrounding, confounding, to bait and betray
And tempt them to battle the sea's width away.

The pot-bellied merchant foreboding no wrong
With headlight and sidelight he lieth along,
Till, lightless and lightfoot and lurking, leap we
To force him discover his business by sea.

CRUISERS

And when we have wakened the lust of a foe,
To draw him by flight toward our bullies we go,
Till, 'ware of strange smoke stealing nearer, he flies—
Or our bullies close in for to make him good prize.

So, when we have spied on the path of their host,
One flieth to carry that word to the coast;
And, lest by false doubling they turn and go free,
One lieth behind them to follow and see.

Anon we return, being gathered again,
Across the sad valleys all drabbled with rain—
Across the grey ridges all crispèd and curled—
To join the long dance round the curve of the world.

The bitter salt spindrift: the sun-glare likewise:
The moon-track a-quiver bewilders our eyes,
Where, linking and lifting, our sisters we hail
'Twixt wrench of cross-surges or plunge of head-gale.

As maidens awaiting the bride to come forth
Make play with light jestings and wit of no worth,
So, widdershins circling the bride-bed of death,
Each fleereth her neighbour and signeth and saith:—

"What see ye?   Their signals, or levin afar?
"What hear ye?   God's thunder, or guns of our war?

CRUISERS

" What mark ye?   Their smoke, or the cloud-rack
     outblown?
" What chase ye?   Their lights, or the Day-star low
     down?"

So, times past all number deceived by false shows,
Deceiving we cumber the road of our foes,
For this is our virtue: to track and betray;
Preparing great battles the sea's width away.

Now peace is at end and our peoples take heart,
For the laws are clean gone that restrained our art;
Up and down the near headlands and against the far
     wind
We are loosed (O be swift!) to the work of our kind!

THE DESTROYERS

The strength of twice three thousand horse
  That seek the single goal;
The line that holds the rending course,
  The hate that swings the whole:
The stripped hulls, slinking through the gloom,
  At gaze and gone again—
The Brides of Death that wait the groom—
  The Choosers of the Slain!

Offshore where sea and skyline blend
  In rain, the daylight dies;
The sullen, shouldering swells attend
  Night and our sacrifice.
Adown the stricken capes no flare—
  No mark on spit or bar,—
Girdled and desperate we dare
  The blindfold game of war.

13

THE DESTROYERS

Nearer the up-flung beams that spell
  The council of our foes;
Clearer the barking guns that tell
  Their scattered flank to close.
Sheer to the trap they crowd their **way**
  From ports for this unbarred.
Quiet, and count our laden prey,
  The convoy and her guard!

On shoal with scarce a foot below,
  Where rock and islet throng,
Hidden and hushed we watch them **throw**
  Their anxious lights along.
Not here, not here your danger lies—
  (Stare hard, O hooded eyne!)
Save where the dazed rock-pigeons rise
  The lit cliffs give no sign.

Therefore—to break the rest ye seek,
  The Narrow Seas to clear—
Hark to the Syren's whimpering shriek—
  The driven death is here!
Look to your van a league away,—
  What midnight terror stays
The bulk that checks against the spray
  Her crackling tops ablaze?

THE DESTROYERS

Hit, and hard hit!   The blow went home,
   The muffled, knocking stroke—
The steam that overruns the foam—
   The foam that thins to smoke—
The smoke that cloaks the deep aboil—
   The deep that chokes her throes
Till, streaked with ash and sleeked with oil,
   The lukewarm whirlpools close!

A shadow down the sickened wave
   Long since her slayer fled:
But hear their chattering quick-fires rave
   Astern, abeam, ahead!
Panic that shells the drifting spar—
   Loud waste with none to check—
Mad fear that rakes a scornful star
   Or sweeps a consort's deck!

Now, while their silly smoke hangs thick,
   Now ere their wits they find,
Lay in and lance them to the quick—
   Our gallied whales are blind!
Good luck to those that see the end,
   Good-bye to those that drown—
For each his chance as chance shall send—
   And God for all!   *Shut down!*

15

THE DESTROYERS

The strength of twice three thousand horse
   That serve the one command;
The hand that heaves the headlong force,
   The hate that backs the hand:
The doom-bolt in the darkness freed,
   The mine that splits the main;
The white-hot wake, the 'wildering speed—
   The Choosers of the Slain!

WHITE HORSES

Where run your colts at pasture?
  Where hide your mares to breed?
'Mid bergs about the Ice-cap
  Or wove Sargasso weed;
By chartless reef and channel,
  Or crafty coastwise bars,
But most the ocean-meadows
  All purple to the stars!

Who holds the rein upon you?
  The latest gale let free.
What meat is in your mangers?
  The glut of all the sea.
'Twixt tide and tide's returning
  Great store of newly dead,—
The bones of those that faced us,
  And the hearts of those that fled.

17

WHITE HORSES

Afar, offshore and single,
  Some stallion, rearing swift,
Neighs hungry for new fodder,
  And calls us to the drift.
Then down the cloven ridges—
  A million hooves unshod—
Break forth the mad White Horses
  To seek their meat from God!

Girth-deep in hissing water
  Our furious vanguard strains—
Through mist of mighty tramplings
  Roll up the fore-blown manes—
A hundred leagues to leeward,
  Ere yet the deep is stirred,
The groaning rollers carry
  The coming of the herd!

Whose hand may grip your nostrils—
  Your forelock who may hold?
E'en they that use the broads with us
  The riders bred and bold,
That spy upon our matings,
  That rope us where we run—
They know the strong White Horses
  From father unto son.

WHITE HORSES

We breathe about their cradles,
    We race their babes ashore,
We snuff against their thresholds,
    We nuzzle at their door;
By day with stamping squadrons,
    By night in whinnying droves,
Creep up the wise White Horses,
    To call them from their loves.

And come they for your calling?
    No wit of man may save.
They hear the loosed White Horses
    Above their father's grave;
And, kin of those we crippled,
    And, sons of those we slew,
Spur down the wild white riders
    To school the herds anew.

What service have ye paid them,
    Oh jealous steeds and strong?
Save we that throw their weaklings,
    Is none dare work them wrong;
While thick around the homestead
    Our snow-backed leaders graze—
A guard behind their plunder,
    And a veil before their ways.

WHITE HORSES

With march and countermarchings—
　　With weight of wheeling hosts—
Stray mob or bands embattled—
　　We ring the chosen coasts:
And, careless of our clamour
　　That bids the stranger fly,
At peace within our pickets
　　The wild white riders lie.

·　　·　　·　　·　　·

Trust ye the curdled hollows—
　　Trust ye the neighing wind—
Trust ye the moaning ground-swell—
　　Our herds are close behind!
To bray your foeman's armies—
　　To chill and snap his sword—
Trust ye the wild White Horses,
　　The Horses of the Lord!

THE SECOND VOYAGE

WE'VE sent our little Cupids all ashore—
    They were frightened, they were tired, they were
      cold;
Our sails of silk and purple go to store,
    And we've cut away our mast of beaten gold
                    (Foul weather!)
Oh 'tis hemp and singing pine for to stand against the
    brine,
    But Love he is the master as of old!

The sea has shorn our galleries away,
    The salt has soiled our gilding past remede;
Our paint is flaked and blistered by the spray,
    Our sides are half a fathom furred in weed
                    (Foul weather!)
And the doves of Venus fled and the petrels came
    instead,
    But Love he was our master at our need!

THE SECOND VOYAGE

'Was Youth would keep no vigil at the bow,
  'Was Pleasure at the helm too drunk to steer—
We've shipped three able quartermasters now,
  Men call them Custom, Reverence, and Fear
            (Foul weather!)
They are old and scarred and plain, but we'll run no
    risk again
  From any Port o' Paphos mutineer!

We seek no more the tempest for delight,
  We skirt no more the indraught and the shoal—
We ask no more of any day or night
  Than to come with least adventure to our goal
            (Foul weather!)
What we find we needs must brook, but we do not go
    to look,
  Nor tempt the Lord our God that saved us whole!

Yet, caring so, not overly we care
  To brace and trim for every foolish blast,
If the squall be pleased to sweep us unaware,
  He may bellow off to leeward like the last
            (Foul weather!)
We will blame it on the deep (for the watch must
    have their sleep),
  And Love can come and wake us when 'tis past.

THE SECOND VOYAGE

Oh launch them down with music from the beach,
   Oh warp them out with garlands from the quays—
Most resolute—a damsel unto each—
   New prows that seek the old Hesperides !
            (Foul weather !)
Though we know the voyage is vain, yet we see our
   path again
   In the saffroned bridesails scenting all the seas !
            (Foul weather !)

THE DYKES

WE have no heart for the fishing, we have no hand
    for the oar—
All that our fathers taught us of old pleases us now
    no more;
All that our own hearts bid us believe we doubt
    where we do not deny—
There is no proof in the bread we eat or rest in the
    toil we ply.

Look you, our foreshore stretches far through sea-
    gate, dyke, and groin—
Made land all, that our fathers made, where the flats
    and the fairway join.
They forced the sea a sea-league back. They died,
    and their work stood fast.
We were born to peace in the lee of the dykes, but
    the time of our peace is past.

THE DYKES

Far off, the full tide clambers and slips, mouthing and
    testing all,
Nipping the flanks of the water-gates, baying along
    the wall;
Turning the shingle, returning the shingle, changing
    the set of the sand . . .
We are too far from the beach, men say, to know how
    the outworks stand.

So we come down, uneasy, to look, uneasily pacing
    the beach.
These are the dykes our fathers made: we have never
    known a breach.
Time and again has the gale blown by and we were
    not afraid;
Now we come only to look at the dykes—at the dykes
    our fathers made.

O'er the marsh where the homesteads cower apart,
    the harried sunlight flies,
Shifts and considers, wanes and recovers, scatters and
    sickens and dies—
An evil ember bedded in ash—a spark blown west by
    the wind . . .
We are surrendered to-night and the sea—the gale
    and the tide behind!

25

THE DYKES

At the bridge of the lower saltings the cattle gather
and blare,
Roused by the feet of running men, dazed by the lantern glare.
Unbar and let them away for their lives—the levels
drown as they stand,
Where the flood-wash forces the sluices aback and the
ditches deliver inland.

Ninefold deep to the top of the dykes the galloping
breakers stride,
And their overcarried spray is a sea—a sea on the
landward side.
Coming, like stallions they paw with their hooves,
going they snatch with their teeth,
Till the bents and the furze and the sand are dragged
out, and the old-time wattles beneath!

Bid men gather fuel for fire, the tar and the oil and
the tow—
Flame we shall need, not smoke, in the dark if the
riddled sea-banks go.
Bid the ringers watch in the tower (who knows what
the dawn shall prove?)
Each with his rope between his feet and the trembling
bells above.

THE DYKES

Now we can only wait till the day, wait and apportion
    our shame!
These are the dykes our fathers left, but we would
    not look to the same.
Time and again were we warned of the dykes, time
    and again we delayed :
Now, it may fall, we have slain our sons as our fathers
    we have betrayed.

.   .   .   .

Walking along the wreck of the dykes, watching the
    work of the seas,
These were the dykes our fathers made to our great
    profit and ease;
But the peace is gone and the profit is gone, and the
    old sure day withdrawn . . .
That our own houses show as strange when we come
    back in the dawn!

THE SONG OF DIEGO VALDEZ

THE God of Fair Beginnings
    Hath prospered here my hand—
The cargoes of my lading,
    And the keels of my command.
For out of many ventures
    That sailed with hope as high,
My own have made the better trade,
    And Admiral am I!

To me my King's much honour,
    To me my people's love—
To me the pride of Princes
    And power all pride above;
To me the shouting cities,
    To me the mob's refrain:—
" Who knows not noble Valdez,
    Hath never heard of Spain."

28

But I remember comrades—
Old playmates on new seas—
Whenas we traded orpiment
Among the savages—
A thousand leagues to south'ard
And thirty years removed—
They knew not noble Valdez,
But me they knew and loved.

Then they that found good liquor,
They drank it not alone,
And they that found fair plunder,
They told us every one,
Behind our chosen islands
Or secret shoals between,
When, walty from far voyage,
We gathered to careen.

There burned our breaming-fagots
All pale along the shore:
There rose our worn pavilions—
A sail above an oar:
As flashed each yearning anchor
Through mellow seas afire,
So swift our careless captains
Rowed each to his desire!

29

THE SONG OF DIEGO VALDEZ

Where lay our loosened harness?
　　Where turned our naked feet?
Whose tavern 'mid the palm-trees?
　　What quenchings of what heat?
Oh fountain in the desert!
　　Oh cistern in the waste!
Oh bread we ate in secret!
　　Oh cup we spilled in haste!

The youth new-taught of longing,
　　The widow curbed and wan—
The goodwife proud at season,
　　And the maid aware of man;
All souls unslaked, consuming,
　　Defrauded in delays,
Desire not more than quittance
　　Than I those forfeit days!

I dreamed to wait my pleasure
　　Unchanged my spring would bide:
Wherefore, to wait my pleasure,
　　I put my spring aside
Till, first in face of Fortune,
　　And last in mazed disdain,
I made Diego Valdez
　　High Admiral of Spain.

THE SONG OF DIEGO VALDEZ

Then walked no wind 'neath Heaven
    Nor surge that did not aid—
I dared extreme occasion,
    Nor ever one betrayed.
They wrought a deeper treason—
    (Led seas that served my needs!)
They sold Diego Valdez
    To bondage of great deeds.

The tempest flung me seaward,
    And pinned and bade me hold
The course I might not alter—
    And men esteemed me bold!
The calms embayed my quarry,
    The fog-wreath sealed his eyes;
The dawn-wind brought my topsails—
    And men esteemed me wise!

Yet 'spite my tyrant triumphs
    Bewildered, dispossessed—
My dream held I before me—
    My vision of my rest;
But, crowned by Fleet and People,
    And bound by King and Pope—
Stands here Diego Valdez
    To rob me of my hope!

31

THE SONG OF DIEGO VALDEZ

No prayer of mine shall move him,
  No word of his set free
The Lord of Sixty Pennants
  And the Steward of the Sea.
His will can loose ten thousand
  To seek their loves again—
But not Diego Valdez,
  High Admiral of Spain.

There walks no wind 'neath Heaven
  Nor wave that shall restore
The old careening riot
  And the clamorous, crowded shore—
The fountain in the desert,
  The cistern in the waste,
The bread we ate in secret,
  The cup we spilled in haste!

Now call I to my Captains—
  For council fly the sign,
Now leap their zealous galleys
  Twelve-oared across the brine.
To me the straiter prison,
  To me the heavier chain—
To me Diego Valdez,
  High Admiral of Spain!

THE BROKEN MEN

FOR things we never mention,
  For Art misunderstood—
For excellent intention
  That did not turn to good;
From ancient tales' renewing,
  From clouds we would not clear—
Beyond the Law's pursuing
  We fled, and settled here.

We took no tearful leaving,
  We bade no long good-byes;
Men talked of crime and thieving,
  Men wrote of fraud and lies.
To save our injured feelings
  'Twas time and time to go—
Behind was dock and Dartmoor,
  Ahead lay Callao!

33

THE BROKEN MEN

The widow and the orphan
    That pray for ten per cent.,
They clapped their trailers on us
    To spy the road we went.
They watched the foreign sailings
    (They scan the shipping still),
And that's your Christian people
    Returning good for ill!

God bless the thoughtful islands
    Where never warrants come!
God bless the just Republics
    That give a man a home,
That ask no foolish questions,
    But set him on his feet;
And save his wife and daughters
    From the workhouse and the street!

On church and square and market
    The noonday silence falls;
You'll hear the drowsy mutter
    Of the fountain in our halls.
Asleep amid the yuccas
    The city takes her ease—
Till twilight brings the land-wind
    To our clicking jalousies.

THE BROKEN MEN

Day long the diamond weather,
  The high, unaltered blue—
The smell of goats and incense
  And the mule-bells tinkling through.
Day long the warder ocean
  That keeps us from our kin,
And once a month our levee
  When the English mail comes in.

You'll find us up and waiting
  To treat you at the bar;
You'll find us less exclusive
  Than the average English are.
We'll meet you with our carriage,
  Too glad to show you round,
But—we do not lunch on steamers,
  For they are English ground.

We sail o' nights to England
  And join our smiling Boards;
Our wives go in with Viscounts
  And our daughters dance with Lords.
But behind our princely doings,
  And behind each coup we make,
We feel there's Something Waiting,
  And—we meet It when we wake.

THE BROKEN MEN

Ah God! One sniff of England—
  To greet our flesh and blood—
To hear the hansoms slurring
  Once more through London mud!
Our towns of wasted honour—
  Our streets of lost delight!
How stands the old Lord Warden?
  Are Dover's cliffs still white?

THE FEET OF THE YOUNG MEN

Now the Four-way Lodge is opened, now the
    Hunting Winds are loose—
Now the Smokes of Spring go up to clear the brain;
Now the Young Men's hearts are troubled for the
    whisper of the Trues,
    Now the Red Gods make their medicine again!
Who hath seen the beaver busied? Who hath
    watched the black-tail mating?
Who hath lain alone to hear the wild-goose cry?
Who hath worked the chosen water where the
    ouananiche is waiting,
    Or the sea-trout's jumping-crazy for the fly?

He must go — go — go away from here!
*   On the other side the world he's overdue.*
'Send your road is clear before you when the old
*   Spring-fret comes o'er you*
*   And the Red Gods call for you!*

THE FEET OF THE YOUNG MEN

So for one the wet sail arching through the rainbow
    round the bow,
And for one the creak of snow-shoes on the crust;
And for one the lakeside lilies where the bull-moose
    waits the cow,
And for one the mule-train coughing in the dust.
Who hath smelt wood-smoke at twilight? Who hath
    heard the birch-log burning?
Who is quick to read the noises of the night?
Let him follow with the others, for the Young Men's
    feet are turning
    To the camps of proved desire and known delight!

    Let him go—go, etc.

I

Do you know the blackened timber—do you know
    that racing stream
    With the raw, right-angled log-jam at the end;
And the bar of sun-warmed shingle where a man
    may bask and dream
    To the click of shod canoe-poles round the bend?
It is there that we are going with our rods and reels
    and traces,
    To a silent smoky Indian that we know—
To a couch of new-pulled hemlock with the starlight
    on our faces,
    For the Red Gods call us out and we must go!

    They must go—go, etc.

38

THE FEET OF THE YOUNG MEN

II

Do you know the shallow Baltic where the seas are
    steep and short,
    Where the bluff, lee-boarded fishing-luggers
    ride?
Do you know the joy of threshing leagues to leeward
    of your port
    On a coast you've lost the chart of overside?
It is there that I am going, with an extra hand to
    bale her—
    Just one able 'long-shore loafer that I know.
He can take his chance of drowning, while I sail and
    sail and sail her,
    For the Red Gods call me out and I must go!

He must go—go, etc.

III

Do you know the pile-built village where the sago-
    dealers trade—
    Do you know the reek of fish and wet bamboo?
Do you know the steaming stillness of the orchid-
    scented glade
    When the blazoned, bird-winged butterflies flap
    through?

39

THE FEET OF THE YOUNG MEN

It is there that I am going with my camphor, net,
 and boxes,
  To a gentle, yellow pirate that I know—
To my little wailing lemurs, to my palms and flying-
 foxes,
  For the Red Gods call me out and I must go!

He must go—go, etc.

IV

Do you know the world's white roof-tree—do you
 know that windy rift
  Where the baffling mountain eddies chop and
   change?
Do you know the long day's patience, belly-down on
 frozen drift,
  While the head of heads is feeding out of range?
It is there that I am going, where the boulders and
 the snow lie,
  With a trusty, nimble tracker that I know.
I have sworn an oath, to keep it on the Horns of
 Ovis Poli,
  And the Red Gods call me out and I must go!

He must go—go, etc.

THE FEET OF THE YOUNG MEN

Now the Four-way Lodge is opened—now the
    Smokes of Council rise—
    Pleasant smokes, ere yet 'twixt trail and trail they
      choose—
Now the girths and ropes are tested: now they pack
    their last supplies:
    Now our Young Men go to dance before the
      Trues!
Who shall meet them at those altars—who shall
    light them to that shrine?
    Velvet-footed, who shall guide them to their goal?
Unto each the voice and vision: unto each his spoor
    and sign—
Lonely mountain in the Northland, misty sweat-bath
    'neath the Line—
    And to each a man that knows his naked soul!

White or yellow, black or copper, he is waiting, as a
    lover,
    Smoke of funnel, dust of hooves, or beat of train—
Where the high grass hides the horseman or the
    glaring flats discover—
Where the steamer hails the landing, or the surf-
    boat brings the rover—
Where the rails run out in sand-drift . . . Quick!
    ah, heave the camp-kit over!
    For the Red Gods make their medicine again!

THE FEET OF THE YOUNG MEN

And we go—go—go away from here!
On the other side the world we're overdue!
'Send the road is clear before you when the old
    Spring-fret comes o'er you
And the Red Gods call for you!

THE TRUCE OF THE BEAR

YEARLY, with tent and rifle, our careless white men
  go
By the pass called Muttianee, to shoot in the vale
  below.
Yearly by Muttianee he follows our white men in—
Matun, the old blind beggar, bandaged from brow
  to chin.

Eyeless, noseless, and lipless—toothless, broken of
  speech,
Seeking a dole at the doorway he mumbles his tale
  to each;
Over and over the story, ending as he began:
" Make ye no truce with Adam-zad—the Bear that
  walks like a man!

" There was a flint in my musket—pricked and
  primed was the pan,
When I went hunting Adam-zad—the Bear that
  stands like a man.

43

THE TRUCE OF THE BEAR

I looked my last on the timber, I looked my last on
the snow,
When I went hunting Adam-zad fifty summers ago!

" I knew his times and his seasons, as he knew mine,
that fed
By night in the ripened maize-field and robbed my
house of bread;
I knew his strength and cunning, as he knew mine,
that crept
At dawn to the crowded goat-pens and plundered
while I slept.

" Up from his stony playground—down from his
well-digged lair—
Out on the naked ridges ran Adam-zad the Bear;
Groaning, grunting, and roaring, heavy with stolen
meals,
Two long marches to northward, and I was at his heels!

" Two full marches to northward, at the fall of the
second night,
I came on mine enemy Adam-zad all panting from
his flight.
There was a charge in the musket—pricked and
primed was the pan—
My finger crooked on the trigger—when he reared
up like a man.

44

THE TRUCE OF THE BEAR

" Horrible, hairy, human, with paws like hands in
 prayer,
Making his supplication rose Adam-zad the Bear!
I looked at the swaying shoulders, at the paunch's
 swag and swing,
And my heart was touched with pity for the monstrous, pleading thing.

" Touched with pity and wonder, I did not fire
 then . . .
I have looked no more on women—I have walked
 no more with men.
Nearer he tottered and nearer, with paws like hands
 that pray—
From brow to jaw that steel-shod paw, it ripped my
 face away!

"Sudden, silent, and savage, searing as flame the blow—
Faceless I fell before his feet, fifty summers ago.
I heard him grunt and chuckle—I heard him pass to
 his den,
He left me blind to the darkened years and the little
 mercy of men.

" Now ye go down in the morning with guns of the
 newer style,
That load (I have felt) in the middle and range (I
 have heard) a mile?

THE TRUCE OF THE BEAR

Luck to the white man's rifle, that shoots so fast and
true,
But—pay, and I lift my bandage and show what the
Bear can do!"

(Flesh like slag in the furnace, knobbed and with-
ered and grey —
Matun, the old blind beggar, he gives good worth
for his pay.)
" Rouse him at noon in the bushes, follow and press
him hard—
Not for his ragings and roarings flinch ye from
Adam-zad.

" But (pay, and I put back the bandage) this is the
time to fear,
When he stands up like a tired man, tottering near
and near;
When he stands up as pleading, in wavering, man-
brute guise,
When he veils the hate and cunning of the little,
swinish eyes;

" When he shows as seeking quarter, with paws like
hands in prayer,
That is the time of peril—the time of the Truce of
the Bear!"

46

THE TRUCE OF THE BEAR

Eyeless, noseless, and lipless, asking a dole at the
    door,
Matun, the old blind beggar, he tells it o'er and o'er;
Fumbling and feeling the rifles, warming his hands at
    the flame,
Hearing our careless white men talk of the morrow's
    game;

Over and over the story, ending as he began: —
*" There is no truce with Adam-zad, the Bear that
    looks like a man! "*

THE OLD MEN

*This is our lot if we live so long and labour unto the
    end —*
*That we outlive the impatient years and the much too
    patient friend :*
*And because we know we have breath in our mouth
    and think we have thought in our head,*
*We shall assume that we are alive, whereas we are
    really dead.*

We shall not acknowledge that old stars fade or alien
    planets arise
(That the sere bush buds or the desert blooms or the
    ancient well-head dries),
Or any new compass wherewith new men adventure
    'neath new skies.

We shall lift up the ropes that constrained our youth
    to bind on our children's hands ;
We shall call to the water below the bridges to re-
    turn and replenish our lands ;
We shall harness horses (Death's own pale horses)
    and scholarly plough the sands.

THE OLD MEN

We shall lie down in the eye of the sun for lack of a
    light on our way —
We shall rise up when the day is done and chirrup,
    "Behold, it is day!"
We shall abide till the battle is won ere we amble
    into the fray.

We shall peck out and discuss and dissect, and evert
    and extrude to our mind,
The flaccid tissues of long-dead issues offensive to
    God and mankind—
(Precisely like vultures over an ox that the Army
    has left behind).

We shall make walk preposterous ghosts of the glo-
    ries we once created—
(Immodestly smearing from muddled palettes amaz-
    ing pigments mismated)
And our friends will weep when we ask them with
    boasts if our natural force be abated.

The Lamp of our Youth will be utterly out: but we
    shall subsist on the smell of it,
And whatever we do, we shall fold our hands and
    suck our gums and think well of it.
Yes, we shall be perfectly pleased with our work,
    and that is the perfectest Hell of it!

THE OLD MEN

*This is our lot if we live so long and listen to those
who love us—
That we are shunned by the people about and shamed
by the Powers above us.
Wherefore be free of your harness betimes ; but being
free be assured,
That he who hath not endured to the death, from his
birth he hath never endured!*

THE EXPLORER

"THERE'S no sense in going further—it's the edge
    of cultivation,"
So they said, and I believed it—broke my land and
    sowed my crop—
Built my barns and strung my fences in the little
    border station
Tucked away below the foothills where the trails run
    out and stop.

Till a voice, as bad as Conscience, rang interminable
    changes
On one everlasting Whisper day and night repeated
    —so:
"Something hidden.   Go and find it.   Go and look
    behind the Ranges—
"Something lost behind the Ranges.   Lost and wait-
    ing for you.   Go!"

THE EXPLORER

So I went, worn out of patience; 'never told my
    nearest neighbours—
Stole away with pack and ponies—left 'em drinking
    in the town;
And the faith that moveth mountains didn't seem to
    help my labours
As I faced the sheer main-ranges, whipping up and
    leading down.

March by march I puzzled through 'em, turning
    flanks and dodging shoulders,
Hurried on in hope of water, headed back for lack of
    grass;
Till I camped above the tree-line—drifted snow and
    naked boulders—
Felt free air astir to windward—knew I'd stumbled
    on the Pass.

'Thought to name it for the finder: but that night
    the Norther found me—
Froze and killed the plains-bred ponies: so I called
    the camp Despair
(It's the Railway Gap to-day, though). Then my
    Whisper waked to hound me:—
"Something lost behind the Ranges. Over yonder.
    Go you there!"

THE EXPLORER

Then I knew, the while I doubted—knew His Hand
was certain o'er me.
Still—it might be self-delusion—scores of better men
had died—
I could reach the township living, but . . . He
knows what terrors tore me . . .
But I didn't . . . but I didn't. I went down the
other side.

Till the snow ran out in flowers, and the flowers
turned to aloes,
And the aloes sprung to thickets and a brimming
stream ran by;
But the thickets dwined to thorn-scrub, and the
water drained to shallows—
And I dropped again on desert, blasted earth, and
blasting sky. . . .

I remember lighting fires; I remember sitting by
them;
I remember seeing faces, hearing voices through the
smoke;
I remember they were fancy—for I threw a stone to
try 'em.
"Something lost behind the Ranges," was the only
word they spoke.

THE EXPLORER

I remember going crazy.   I remember that I knew
    it
When I heard myself hallooing to the funny folk I
    saw.
Very full of dreams that desert: but my two legs
    took me through it . . .
And I used to watch 'em moving with the toes all
    black and raw.

But at last the country altered—White man's country
    past disputing—
Rolling grass and open timber, with a hint of hills
    behind—
There I found me food and water, and I lay a week
    recruiting,
Got my strength and lost my nightmares.   Then I
    entered on my find.

Thence I ran my first rough survey—chose my trees
    and blazed and ringed 'em—
Week by week I pried and sampled—week by week
    my findings grew.
Saul he went to look for donkeys, and by God he
    found a kingdom!
But by God, who sent His Whisper, I had struck the
    worth of two!

THE EXPLORER

Up along the hostile mountains, where the hair-
    poised snow-slide shivers—
Down and through the big fat marshes that the
    virgin ore-bed stains,
Till I heard the mile-wide mutterings of unimagined
    rivers,
And beyond the nameless timber saw illimitable
    plains!

'Plotted sites of future cities, traced the easy grades
    between 'em;
Watched unharnessed rapids wasting fifty thousand
    head an hour;
Counted leagues of water-frontage through the axe-
    ripe woods that screen 'em—
Saw the plant to feed a people—up and waiting for
    the power!

Well I know who'll take the credit—all the clever
    chaps that followed—
Came, a dozen men together—never knew my desert
    fears;
Tracked me by the camps I'd quitted, used the water-
    holes I'd hollowed.
They'll go back and do the talking. They'll be
    called the Pioneers!

THE EXPLORER

They will find my sites of townships—not the cities
    that I set there.
They will rediscover rivers—not my rivers heard at
    night.
By my own old marks and bearings they will show
    me how to get there,
By the lonely cairns I builded they will guide my
    feet aright.

Have I named one single river? Have I claimed one
    single acre?
Have I kept one single nugget—(barring samples)?
    No, not I.
Because my price was paid me ten times over by my
    Maker.
But you wouldn't understand it. You go up and
    occupy.

Ores you'll find there; wood and cattle; water-
    transit sure and steady
(That should keep the railway rates down), coal and
    iron at your doors.
God took care to hide that country till He judged
    His people ready,
Then He chose me for His Whisper, and I've found
    it, and it's yours!

THE EXPLORER

Yes, your "Never-never country"—yes, your "edge
  of cultivation"

And "no sense in going further"—till I crossed the
  range to see.

God forgive me! No, *I* didn't. It's God's present
  to our nation.

Anybody might have found it but—His Whisper
  came to Me!

THE WAGE-SLAVES

OH glorious are the guarded heights
 Where guardian souls abide—
Self-exiled from our gross delights—
 Above, beyond, outside:
An ampler arc their spirit swings—
 Commands a juster view—
We have their word for all these things,
 Nor doubt their words are true.

Yet we the bondslaves of our day,
 Whom dirt and danger press—
Co-heirs of insolence, delay,
 And leagued unfaithfulness—
Such is our need must seek indeed
 And, having found, engage
The men who merely do the work
 For which they draw the wage.

58

THE WAGE-SLAVES

From forge and farm and mine and bench,
   Deck, altar, outpost lone—
Mill, school, battalion, counter, trench,
   Rail, senate, sheepfold, throne—
Creation's cry goes up on high
   From age to cheated age:
" Send us the men who do the work
   For which they draw the wage."

Words cannot help nor wit achieve,
   Nor e'en the all-gifted fool,
Too weak to enter, bide, or leave
   The lists he cannot rule.
Beneath the sun we count on none
   Our evil to assuage,
Except the men that do the work
   For which they draw the wage.

When through the Gates of Stress and Strain
   Comes forth the vast Event—
The simple, sheer, sufficing, sane
   Result of labour spent—
They that have wrought the end unthought
   Be neither saint nor sage,
But men who merely did the work
   For which they drew the wage.

THE WAGE-SLAVES

Wherefore to these the Fates shall bend
   (And all old idle things—)
Wherefore on these shall Power attend
   Beyond the grasp of kings:
Each in his place, by right, not grace,
   Shall rule his heritage—
The men who simply do the work
   For which they draw the wage.

Not such as scorn the loitering street,
   Or waste, to earn its praise,
Their noontide's unreturning heat
   About their morning ways:
But such as dower each mortgaged hour
   Alike with clean courage—
Even the men who do the work
   For which they draw the wage—
Men like to Gods that do the work
   For which they draw the wage—
Begin—continue—close the work
   For which they draw the wage!

THE BURIAL

C. J. RHODES, buried in the Matoppos, April 10, 1902

WHEN that great Kings return to clay,
  Or Emperors in their pride,
Grief of a day shall fill a day,
  Because its creature died.
But we—we reckon not with those
  Whom the mere Fates ordain,
This Power that wrought on us and goes
  Back to the Power again.

Dreamer devout, by vision led
  Beyond our guess or reach,
The travail of his spirit bred
  Cities in place of speech.
So huge the all-mastering thought that
    drove—
  So brief the term allowed—
Nations, not words, he linked to prove
  His faith before the crowd.

THE BURIAL

It is his will that he look forth
  Across the world he won—
The granite of the ancient North—
  Great spaces washed with sun.
There shall he patient make his seat
  (As when the Death he dared),
And there await a people's feet
  In the paths that he prepared.

There, till the vision he foresaw
  Splendid and whole arise,
And unimagined Empires draw
  To council 'neath his skies,
The immense and brooding Spirit still
  Shall quicken and control.
Living he was the land, and dead,
  His soul shall be her soul!

GENERAL JOUBERT

(Died March 27, 1900)

WITH those that bred, with those that loosed the
    strife,
  He had no part whose hands were clear of gain;
But subtle, strong, and stubborn, gave his life
  To a lost cause, and knew the gift was vain.

Later shall rise a people, sane and great,
  Forged in strong fires, by equal war made one;
Telling old battles over without hate—
  Not least his name shall pass from sire to son.

He may not meet the onsweep of our van
  In the doomed city when we close the score.
Yet o'er his grave—his grave that holds a man—
  Our deep-tongued guns shall answer his once
    more!

THE PALACE

WHEN I was a King and a Mason—a Master proven
and skilled—
I cleared me ground for a palace such as a King
should build.
I decreed and dug down to my levels.   Presently,
under the silt,
I came on the wreck of a palace such as a King had
built.

There was no worth in the fashion—there was no wit
in the plan—
Hither and thither, aimless, the ruined footings
ran—
Masonry, brute, mishandled, but carven on every
stone:
"*After me cometh a Builder.   Tell him, I too have
known.*"

THE PALACE

Swift to my use in my trenches, where my well-
planned ground-works grew,
I tumbled his quoins and his ashlars, and cut and
reset them anew.
Lime I milled of the marbles; burned it, slacked it,
and spread;
Taking and leaving at pleasure the gifts of the
humble dead.

Yet I despised not nor gloried; yet, as we wrenched
them apart,
I read in the razed foundations the heart of that
builder's heart.
As he had risen and pleaded, so did I understand
The form of the dream he had followed in the face of
the thing he had planned.

.   .   .   .

When I was a King and a Mason—in the open noon
of my pride,
They sent me a Word from the Darkness—They
whispered and put me aside.
They said—" The end is forbidden."   They said—
"Thy use is fulfilled,
"And thy palace shall stand as that other's—the
spoil of a King who shall build."

THE PALACE

I called my men from my trenches, my quarries, my
    wharves, and my shears.
All I had wrought I abandoned to the faith of the
    faithless years.
Only I cut on the timber, only I carved on the
    stone:
After me cometh a Builder.   Tell him, I too have
    known!

SUSSEX

God gave all men all earth to love,
    But since our hearts are small,
Ordained for each one spot should prove
    Beloved over all;
That as He watched Creation's birth,
    So we, in godlike mood,
May of our love create our earth
    And see that it is good.

So one shall Baltic pines content,
    As one some Surrey glade,
Or one the palm-grove's droned lament
    Before Levuka's trade.
Each to his choice, and I rejoice
    The lot has fallen to me
In a fair ground—in a fair ground—
    Yea, Sussex by the sea!

SUSSEX

No tender-hearted garden crowns,
   No bosomed woods adorn
Our blunt, bow-headed, whale-backed Downs,
   But gnarled and writhen thorn—
Fair slopes where chasing shadows skim,
   And through the gaps revealed
Belt upon belt, the wooded, dim
   Blue goodness of the Weald.

Clean of officious fence or hedge,
   Half-wild and wholly tame,
The wise turf cloaks the white cliff edge
   As when the Romans came.
What sign of those that fought and died
   At shift of sword and sword?
The barrow and the camp abide,
   The sunlight and the sward.

Here leaps ashore the full Sou'west
   All heavy-winged with brine,
Here lies above the folded crest
   The Channel's leaden line;
And here the sea-fogs lap and cling,
   And here, each warning each,
The sheep-bells and the ship-bells ring
   Along the hidden beach.

SUSSEX

We have no waters to delight
    Our broad and brookless vales—
Only the dewpond on the height
    Unfed, that never fails,
Whereby no tattered herbage tells
    Which way the season flies—
Only our close-bit thyme that smells
    Like dawn in Paradise.

Here through the strong unhampered days
    The tinkling silence thrills;
Or little, lost, Down churches praise
    The Lord who made the hills:
But here the Old Gods guard their round,
    And, in her secret heart,
The heathen kingdom Wilfrid found
    Dreams, as she dwells, apart.

Though all the rest were all my share,
    With equal soul I'd see
Her nine-and-thirty sisters fair,
    Yet none more fair than she.
Choose ye your need from Thames to Tweed,
    And I will choose instead
Such lands as lie 'twixt Rake and Rye,
    Black Down and Beachy Head.

SUSSEX

I will go out against the sun
  Where the rolled scarp retires,
And the Long Man of Wilmington
  Looks naked toward the shires;
And east till doubling Rother crawls
  To find the fickle tide,
By dry and sea-forgotten walls,
  Our ports of stranded pride.

I will go north about the shaws
  And the deep ghylls that breed
Huge oaks and old, the which we hold
  No more than " Sussex weed ";
Or south where windy Piddinghoe's
  Begilded dolphin veers,
And black beside wide-bankèd Ouse
  Lie down our Sussex steers.

So to the land our hearts we give
  Till the sure magic strike,
And Memory, Use, and Love make live
  Us and our fields alike—
That deeper than our speech and thought,
  Beyond our reason's sway,
Clay of the pit whence we were wrought
  Yearns to its fellow-clay.

SUSSEX

God gives all men all earth to love,
*   But since man's heart is small,*
Ordains for each one spot shall prove
*   Beloved over all.*
Each to his choice, and I rejoice
*   The lot has fallen to me*
In a fair ground—in a fair ground—
*   Yea, Sussex by the sea!*

SONG OF THE WISE CHILDREN

WHEN the darkened Fifties dip to the North,
  And frost and the fog divide the air,
And the day is dead at his breaking-forth,
  Sirs, it is bitter beneath the Bear!

Far to Southward they wheel and glance,
  The million molten spears of morn—
The spears of our deliverance
  That shine on the house where we were born.

Flying-fish about our bows,
  Flying sea-fires in our wake:
This is the road to our Father's House,
  Whither we go for our soul's sake!

SONG OF THE WISE CHILDREN

We have forfeited our birthright,
    We have forsaken all things meet;
We have forgotten the look of light,
    We have forgotten the scent of heat.

They that walk with shaded brows,
    Year by year in a shining land,
They be men of our Father's House,
    They shall receive us and understand.

We shall go back by boltless doors,
    To the life unaltered our childhood knew—
To the naked feet on the cool, dark floors,
    And the high-ceiled rooms that the Trade blows
        through:

To the trumpet-flowers and the moon beyond,
    And the tree-toad's chorus drowning all—
And the lisp of the split banana-frond
    That talked us to sleep when we were small.

The wayside magic, the threshold spells,
    Shall soon undo what the North has done—
Because of the sights and the sounds and the smells
    That ran with our youth in the eye of the sun!

73

SONG OF THE WISE CHILDREN

And Earth accepting shall ask no vows,
  Nor the Sea our love nor our lover the Sky.
When we return to our Father's House
  Only the English shall wonder why!

BUDDHA AT KAMAKURA

" And there is a Japanese idol at Kamakura."

OH ye who tread the Narrow Way
By Tophet-flare to Judgment Day,
Be gentle when the " heathen " pray
   To Buddha at Kamakura!

To him the Way, the Law, Apart,
Whom Maya held beneath her heart,
Ananda's Lord the Bodhisat,
   The Buddha of Kamakura.

For though he neither burns nor sees,
Nor hears ye thank your Deities,
Ye have not sinned with such as these,
   His children at Kamakura;

BUDDHA AT KAMAKURA

Yet spare us still the Western joke
When joss-sticks turn to scented smoke
The little sins of little folk
    That worship at Kamakura—

The grey-robed, gay-sashed butterflies
That flit beneath the Master's eyes—
He is beyond the Mysteries
    But loves them at Kamakura.

And whoso will, from Pride released,
Contemning neither creed nor priest,
May feel the soul of all the East
    About him at Kamakura.

Yea, every tale Ananda heard,
Of birth as fish or beast or bird,
While yet in lives the Master stirred,
    The warm wind brings Kamakura.

Till drowsy eyelids seem to see
A-flower 'neath her golden *htee*
The Shwe-Dagon flare easterly
    From Burmah to Kamakura.

BUDDHA AT KAMAKURA

And down the loaded air there comes
The thunder of Thibetan drums,
And droned—" *Om mane padme oms* "—
  A world's width from Kamakura.

Yet Brahmans rule Benares still,
Buddh-Gaya's ruins pit the hill,
And beef-fed zealots threaten ill
  To Buddha and Kamakura.

A tourist-show, a legend told,
A rusting bulk of bronze and gold,
So much, and scarce so much, ye hold
  The meaning of Kamakura?

But when the morning prayer is prayed,
Think, ere ye pass to strife and trade,
Is God in human image made
  No nearer than Kamakura?

THE WHITE MAN'S BURDEN

TAKE up the White Man's burden—
   Send forth the best ye breed—
Go bind your sons to exile
   To serve your captives' need;
To wait in heavy harness,
   On fluttered folk and wild—
Your new-caught, sullen peoples,
   Half-devil and half-child.

Take up the White Man's burden—
   In patience to abide,
To veil the threat of terror
   And check the show of pride;
By open speech and simple,
   An hundred times made plain,
To seek another's profit,
   And work another's gain.

THE WHITE MAN'S BURDEN

Take up the White Man's burden—
 The savage wars of peace—
Fill full the mouth of Famine
 And bid the sickness cease.
And when your goal is nearest
 The end for others sought,
Watch Sloth and heathen Folly
 Bring all your hope to naught.

Take up the White Man's burden—
 No tawdry rule of kings,
But toil of serf and sweeper—
 The tale of common things.
The ports ye shall not enter,
 The roads ye shall not tread,
Go make them with your living,
 And mark them with your dead.

Take up the White Man's burden—
 And reap his old reward:
The blame of those ye better,
 The hate of those ye guard—
The cry of hosts ye humour
 (Ah, slowly!) toward the light:—
"Why brought ye us from bondage,
 Our loved Egyptian night?"

THE WHITE MAN'S BURDEN

Take up the White Man's burden—
　　Ye dare not stoop to less—
Nor call too loud on Freedom
　　To cloak your weariness;
By all ye cry or whisper,
　　By all ye leave or do,
The silent, sullen peoples
　　Shall weigh your Gods and you.

Take up the White Man's burden—
　　Have done with childish days—
The lightly proffered laurel,
　　The easy, ungrudged praise.
Comes now, to search your manhood
　　Through all the thankless years,
Cold, edged with dear-bought wisdom,
　　The judgment of your peers!

PHARAOH AND THE SERGEANT

" . . . Consider that the meritorious services of the Sergeant Instructors attached to the Egyptian Army have been inadequately acknowledged. . . . To the excellence of their work is mainly due the great improvement that has taken place in the soldiers of H. H. the Khedive."

Extract from letter.

SAID England unto Pharaoh, " I must make a man
    of you,
  That will stand upon his feet and play the game ;
That will Maxim his oppressor as a Christian ought
    to do,"
  And she sent old Pharaoh Sergeant Whatisname.
    It was not a Duke nor Earl, nor yet a *Vis*count—
      It was not a big brass General that came ;
    But a man in khaki kit who could handle men **a**
      bit,
      With his bedding labelled Sergeant Whatis-
      name.

PHARAOH AND THE SERGEANT

Said England unto Pharaoh, " Though at present
    singing small,
  You shall hum a proper tune before it ends,"
And she introduced old Pharaoh to the Sergeant
    once for all,
    And left 'em in the desert making friends.
      It was not a Crystal Palace nor Cathedral;
        It was not a public-house of common fame;
      But a piece of red-hot sand, with a palm on
        either hand,
        And a little hut for Sergeant Whatisname.

Said England unto Pharaoh, " You've had miracles
    before,
  When Aaron struck your rivers into blood;
But if you watch the Sergeant he can show you
    something more,
    He's a charm for making riflemen from mud."
      It was neither Hindustani, French, nor Coptics;
        It was odds and ends and leavings of the
        same,
      Translated by a stick (which is really half the
        trick),
        And Pharaoh harked to Sergeant Whatis-
        name.

PHARAOH AND THE SERGEANT

(There were years that no one talked of ; there were
    times of horrid doubt—
  There was faith and hope and whacking and
    despair—
While the Sergeant gave the Cautions and he combed
    old Pharaoh out,
  And England didn't seem to know nor care.
    That is England's awful way o' doing business—
      She would serve her God or Gordon just the
        same—
      For she thinks her Empire still is the Strand and
        Holborn Hill,
        And she didn't think of Sergeant Whatis-
          name.)

Said England to the Sergeant, " You can let my
    people go!"
  (England used 'em cheap and nasty from the start),
And they entered 'em in battle on a most astonished
    foe—
  But the Sergeant he had hardened Pharaoh's
    heart.
    That was broke, along of all the plagues of
      Egypt,
      Three thousand years before the Sergeant
        came—

PHARAOH AND THE SERGEANT

And he mended it again in a little more than
ten,
So Pharaoh fought like Sergeant Whatisname!

It was wicked bad campaigning (cheap and nasty
from the first),
There was heat and dust and coolie-work and sun,
There were vipers, flies, and sandstorms, there was
cholera and thirst,
But Pharaoh done the best he ever done.
Down the desert, down the railway, down the
river,
Like Israelites from bondage so he came,
'Tween the clouds o' dust and fire to the land
of his desire,
And his Moses, it was Sergeant Whatisname!

We are eating dirt in handfuls for to save our daily
bread,
Which we have to buy from those that hate us
most,
And we must not raise the money where the Sergeant raised the dead,
And it's wrong and bad and dangerous to boast.

84

PHARAOH AND THE SERGEANT

But he did it on the cheap and on the quiet,
    And he's not allowed to forward any claim—
Though he drilled a black man white, though he
    made a mummy fight,
    He will still continue Sergeant Whatisname—
Private, Corporal, Colour-Sergeant, and In-
    structor—
    But the everlasting miracle's the same!

OUR LADY OF THE SNOWS

(CANADIAN PREFERENTIAL TARIFF, 1897)

A NATION spoke to a Nation,
    A Queen sent word to a Throne:
" Daughter am I in my mother's house,
    But mistress in my own.
The gates are mine to open,
    As the gates are mine to close,
And I set my house in order,"
    Said our Lady of the Snows.

" Neither with laughter nor weeping,
    Fear or the child's amaze—
Soberly under the White Man's law
    My white men go their ways.
Not for the Gentiles' clamour—
    Insult or threat of blows—
Bow we the knee to Baal,"
    Said our Lady of the Snows.

OUR LADY OF THE SNOWS

" My speech is clean and single,
 I talk of common things—
Words of the wharf and the market-place
 And the ware the merchant brings;
Favour to those I favour,
 But a stumbling-block to my foes.
Many there be that hate us,"
 Said our Lady of the Snows.

" I called my chiefs to council
 In the din of a troubled year;
For the sake of a sign ye would not see,
 And a word ye would not hear.
This is our message and answer;
 This is the path we chose:
For we be also a people,"
 Said our Lady of the Snows.

" Carry the word to my sisters—
 To the Queens of the East and the South.
I have proven faith in the Heritage
 By more than the word of the mouth.
They that are wise may follow
 Ere the world's war-trumpet blows:
But I—I am first in the battle,"
 Said our Lady of the Snows.

87

OUR LADY OF THE SNOWS

A Nation spoke to a Nation,
*   A Throne sent word to a Throne:*
" Daughter am I in my mother's house,
*   But mistress in my own !*
The gates are mine to open,
*   As the gates are mine to close,*
And I abide by my mother's house,"
*   Said our Lady of the Snows.*

"ET DONA FERENTES"

IN extended observation of the ways and works of
    man,
From the Four-mile Radius roughly to the plains of
    Hindustan:
I have drunk with mixed assemblies, seen the racial
    ruction rise,
And the men of half creation damning half creation's
    eyes.

I have watched them in their tantrums, all that
    pentecostal crew,
French, Italian, Arab, Spaniard, Dutch and Greek,
    and Russ and Jew,
Celt and savage, buff and ochre, cream and yellow,
    mauve and white,
But it never really mattered till the English grew
    polite;

"ET DONA FERENTES"

Till the men with polished toppers, till the men in
    long frock-coats,
Till the men that do not duel, till the men who fight
    with votes,
Till the breed that take their pleasures as Saint
    Laurence took his grid,
Began to "beg your pardon" and—the knowing
    croupier hid.

Then the bandsmen with their fiddles, and the girls
    that bring the beer,
Felt the psychologic moment, left the lit casino clear;
But the uninstructed alien, from the Teuton to the
    Gaul,
Was entrapped, once more, my country, by that
    suave, deceptive drawl.

   .   .   .   .

As it was in ancient Suez or 'neath wilder, milder
    skies,
I "observe with apprehension" when the racial ruc-
    tions rise;
And with keener apprehension, if I read the times
    aright,
Hear the old casino order: "Watch your man, but
    be polite.

"ET DONA FERENTES"

"Keep your temper. Never answer (*that* was why
    they spat and swore).
Don't hit first, but move together (there's no hurry)
    to the door.
Back to back, and facing outward while the linguist
    tells 'em how—
'*Nous sommes allong à notre batteau, nous ne voulong
    pas un row.*'"

So the hard, pent rage ate inward, till some idiot
    went too far . . .
"Let 'em have it!" and they had it, and the same
    was serious war.
Fist, umbrella, cane, decanter, lamp and beer-mug,
    chair and boot—
Till behind the fleeing legions rose the long, hoarse
    yell for loot.

Then the oil-cloth with its numbers, as a banner
    fluttered free;
Then the grand piano cantered, on three castors,
    down the quay;
White, and breathing through their nostrils, silent,
    systematic, swift—
They removed, effaced, abolished all that man could
    heave or lift.

91

"ET DONA FERENTES"

Oh, my country, bless the training that from cot to
    castle runs—
The pitfall of the stranger but the bulwark of thy
    sons—
Measured speech and ordered action, sluggish soul
    and unperturbed,
Till we wake our Island-Devil—nowise cool for being
    curbed!

When the heir of all the ages " has the honour to
    remain,"
When he will not hear an insult, though men make
    it ne'er so plain,
When his lips are schooled to meekness, when his
    back is bowed to blows—
Well the keen *aas-vogels* know it—well the waiting
    jackal knows.

Build on the flanks of Etna where the sullen smoke-
    puffs float—
Or bathe in tropic waters where the lean fin dogs the
    boat—
Cock the gun that is not loaded, cook the frozen
    dynamite—
But oh, beware my country, when my country grows
    polite!

KITCHENER'S SCHOOL

Being a translation of the song that was made by a Moham-
medan schoolmaster of Bengal Infantry (some time on service
at Suakim) when he heard that the Sirdar was taking money
from the English to build a Madrissa for Hubshees—or a
college for the Sudanese, 1898.

OH Hubshee, carry your shoes in your hand and
    bow your head on your breast!
This is the message of Kitchener who did not break
    you in jest.
It was permitted to him to fulfil the long-appointed
    years,
Reaching the end ordained of old over your dead
    Emirs.

He stamped only before your walls, and the Tomb
    ye knew was dust:
He gathered up under his armpits all the swords of
    your trust:

He set a guard on your granaries, securing the weak
from the strong:
He said:—" Go work the water-wheels that were
abolished so long."

He said:—" Go safely, being abased.   I have
accomplished my vow."
That was the mercy of Kitchener.   Cometh his
madness now!
He does not desire as ye desire, nor devise as ye
devise:
He is preparing a second host—an army to make you
wise.

Not at the mouth of his clean-lipped guns shall ye
learn his name again,
But letter by letter, from Kaf to Kaf, at the mouth
of his chosen men.
He has gone back to his own city, not seeking
presents or bribes,
But openly asking the English for money to buy you
Hakims and scribes.

Knowing that ye are forfeit by battle and have no
right to live,
He begs for money to bring you learning—and all
the English give.

KITCHENER'S SCHOOL

It is their treasure—it is their pleasure—thus are
    their hearts inclined:
For Allah created the English mad—the maddest of
    all mankind!

They do not consider the Meaning of Things; they
    consult not creed nor clan.
Behold, they clap the slave on the back, and behold,
    he ariseth a man!
They terribly carpet the earth with dead, and before
    their cannon cool,
They walk unarmed by twos and threes to call the
    living to school.

How is this reason (which is their reason) to judge a
    scholar's worth,
By casting a ball at three straight sticks and
    defending the same with a fourth?
But this they do (which is doubtless a spell) and
    other matters more strange,
Until, by the operation of years, the hearts of their
    scholars change:

Till these make come and go great boats or engines
    upon the rail
(But always the English watch near by to prop them
    when they fail);

Till these make laws of their own choice and Judges
of their own blood;
And all the mad English obey the Judges and say
that the Law is good.

Certainly they were mad from of old: but I think
one new thing,
That the magic whereby they work their magic—
wherefrom their fortunes spring—
May be that they show all peoples their magic and
ask no price in return.
Wherefore, since ye are bond to that magic, oh
Hubshee, make haste and learn!

Certainly also is Kitchener mad.   But one sure thing
I know—
If he who broke you be minded to teach you, to his
Madrissa go!
Go, and carry your shoes in your hand and bow
your head on your breast,
For he who did not slay you in sport, he will not
teach you in jest.

THE YOUNG QUEEN

(THE COMMONWEALTH OF AUSTRALIA, INAUGURATED
NEW YEAR'S DAY, 1901)

HER hand was still on her sword-hilt, the spur was
    still on her heel,
She had not cast her harness of grey war-dinted
    steel;
High on her red-splashed charger, beautiful, bold,
    and browned,
Bright-eyed out of the battle, the Young Queen
    rode to be crowned.

She came to the Old Queen's presence, in the Hall
    of Our Thousand Years—
In the Hall of the Five Free Nations that are peers
    among their peers:

Copyright, 1900, by Rudyard Kipling.

97

THE YOUNG QUEEN

Royal she gave the greeting, loyal she bowed the
    head,
Crying:—"Crown me, my Mother!" And the Old
    Queen stood and said:—

"How can I crown thee further? I know whose
    standard flies
Where the clean surge takes the Leeuwin or the
    coral barriers rise.
Blood of our foes on thy bridle, and speech of our
    friends in thy mouth—
How can I crown thee further, O Queen of the
    Sovereign South?

"Let the Five Free Nations witness!" But the
    Young Queen answered swift:—
"It shall be crown of Our crowning to hold Our
    crown for a gift.
In the days when Our folk were feeble thy sword
    made sure Our lands:
Wherefore We come in power to take Our crown at
    thy hands."

And the Old Queen raised and kissed her, and the
    jealous circlet prest,
Roped with the pearls of the Northland and red with
    the gold of the West,

THE YOUNG QUEEN

Lit with her land's own opals, levin-hearted, alive,
And the five-starred cross above them, for sign of
  the Nations Five.

So it was done in the Presence—in the Hall of Our
  Thousand Years,
In the face of the Five Free Nations that have no
  peer but their peers;
And the Young Queen out of the Southland kneeled
  down at the Old Queen's knee,
And asked for a mother's blessing on the excellent
  years to be.

And the Old Queen stooped in the stillness where
  the jewelled head drooped low:—
"Daughter no more but Sister, and doubly Daughter
  so—
Mother of many princes—and child of the child I
  bore,
What good thing shall I wish thee that I have not
  wished before?

"Shall I give thee delight in dominion—mere pride
  of thy setting forth?
Nay, we be women together—we know what that
  lust is worth.

THE YOUNG QUEEN

Peace in thy utmost borders, and strength on a road
   untrod?
These are dealt or diminished at the secret will of
   God.

"I have swayed troublous councils, I am wise in
   terrible things;
Father and son and grandson, I have known the
   heart of the Kings.
Shall I give thee my sleepless wisdom, or the gift all
   wisdom above?
Ay, we be women together—I give thee thy people's
   love:

"Tempered, august, abiding, reluctant of prayers or
   vows,
Eager in face of peril as thine for thy mother's house.
God requite thee, my Sister, through the wonderful
   years to be,
And make thy people to love thee as thou hast loved
   me!"

RIMMON

DULY with knees that feign to quake—
　Bent head and shaded brow,—
Yet once again, for my father's sake,
　In Rimmon's House I bow.

The curtains part, and the trumpet blares,
　And the eunuchs howl aloud;
And the gilt, swag-bellied idol glares
　Insolent over the crowd.

" *This is Rimmon, Lord of the Earth—*
　" *Fear Him and bow the knee !* "
And I watch my comrades hide their mirth
　That rode to the wars with me.

For we remember the sun and the sand
　And the rocks whereon we trod,
Ere we came to a scorched and a scornful land
　That did not know our God;

RIMMON

As we remember the sacrifice
  Dead men an hundred laid—
Slain while they served His mysteries
  And that He would not aid.

Not though we gashed ourselves and wept,
  For the high-priest bade us wait;
Saying He went on a journey or slept,
  Or was drunk or had taken a mate.

(Praise ye Rimmon, King of Kings,
  Who ruleth Earth and Sky!
And again I bow as the censer swings
  And the God Enthroned goes by.)

Ay, we remember His sacred ark
  And the virtuous men that knelt
To the dark and the hush behind the dark
  Wherein we dreamed He dwelt;

Until we entered to hale Him out,
  And found no more than an old
Uncleanly image girded about
  The loins with scarlet and gold.

RIMMON

Him we o'erset with the butts of our spears—
  Him and His vast designs—
To be the scorn of our muleteers
  And the jest of our halted lines.

By the picket-pins that the dogs defile,
  In the dung and the dust He lay,
Till the priests ran and chattered awhile
  And wiped Him and took Him away.

Hushing the matter before it was known,
  They returned to our fathers afar,
And hastily set Him afresh on His throne
  Because He had won us the war.

Wherefore with knees that feign to quake—
  Bent head and shaded brow—
To this great dog, for my father's sake,
  In Rimmon's House I bow.

THE OLD ISSUE

(October 9, 1899)

" *Here is nothing new nor aught unproven,*" **say the**
    " *Many feet have worn it and the road is old*
        indeed.
" *It is the King—the King we schooled aforetime!* "
    (Trumpets in the marshes—in the eyot at Runny-
        mede!)

" *Here is neither haste, nor hate, nor anger,*" *peal the*
    Trumpets,
    " *Pardon for his penitence or pity for his fall.*
" *It is the King!* " *—inexorable Trumpets—*
    (Trumpets round the scaffold at the dawning by
        Whitehall!)

104

THE OLD ISSUE

" He hath veiled the crown and hid the sceptre," warn
    the Trumpets,
      " He hath changed the fashion of the lies that cloak
      his will.
" Hard die the Kings—ah hard—dooms hard ! "
    declare the Trumpets,
      Trumpets at the gang-plank where the brawling
      troop-decks fill !

Ancient and Unteachable, abide—abide the Trumpets!
    Once again the Trumpets, for the shuddering
      ground-swell brings
Clamour over ocean of the harsh pursuing Trumpets—
    Trumpets of the Vanguard that have sworn no
      truce with Kings !

All we have of freedom, all we use or know—
This our fathers bought for us long and long ago.

Ancient Right unnoticed as the breath we draw—
Leave to live by no man's leave, underneath the
    Law.

Lance and torch and tumult, steel and grey-goose
    wing
Wrenched it, inch and ell and all, slowly from the
    King.

THE OLD ISSUE

Till our fathers 'stablished, after bloody years,
How our King is one with us, first among his peers.

So they bought us freedom—not at little cost—
Wherefore must we watch the King, lest our gain be
    lost.

Over all things certain, this is sure indeed,
Suffer not the old King: for we know the breed.

Give no ear to bondsmen bidding us endure,
Whining " He is weak and far "; crying " Time shall
    cure."

(Time himself is witness, till the battle joins,
Deeper strikes the rottenness in the people's loins.)

Give no heed to bondsmen masking war with peace.
Suffer not the old King here or overseas!

They that beg us barter—wait his yielding mood—
Pledge the years we hold in trust—pawn our
    brother's blood—

Howso' great their clamour, whatsoe'er their claim,
Suffer not the old King under any name!

Here is naught unproven—here is naught to learn.
It is written what shall fall if the King return.

THE OLD ISSUE

He shall mark our goings, question whence we came,
Set his guards about us, as in Freedom's name.

He shall take a tribute, toll of all our ware;
He shall change our gold for arms—arms we may
    not bear.

He shall break his Judges if they cross his word;
He shall rule above the Law calling on the Lord.

He shall peep and mutter; and the night shall bring
Watchers 'neath our window, lest we mock the
    King—

Hate and all division; hosts of hurrying spies;
Money poured in secret, carrion breeding flies.

Strangers of his council, hirelings of his pay,
These shall deal our Justice: sell—deny—delay.

We shall drink dishonour, we shall eat abuse
For the Land we look to—for the Tongue we use.

We shall take our station, dirt beneath his feet,
While his hired captains jeer us in the street.

Cruel in the shadow, crafty in the sun,
Far beyond his borders shall his teachings run.

THE OLD ISSUE

Sloven, sullen, savage, secret, uncontrolled—
Laying on a new land evil of the old;

Long-forgotten bondage, dwarfing heart and brain—
All our fathers died to loose he shall bind again.

Here is naught at venture, random nor untrue—
Swings the wheel full-circle, brims the cup anew.

Here is naught unproven, here is nothing hid:
Step for step and word for word—so the old Kings
      did!

Step by step and word by word: who is ruled may
      read.
Suffer not the old Kings—for we know the breed—

All the right they promise—all the wrong they bring.
Stewards of the Judgment, suffer not this King!

BRIDGE-GUARD IN THE KARROO

"and will supply details to guard the Blood River Bridge."
District Orders—Lines of Communication.

SUDDEN the desert changes,
    The raw glare softens and clings,
Till the aching Oudtshoorn ranges
    Stand up like the thrones of kings—

Ramparts of slaughter and peril—
    Blazing, amazing—aglow
'Twixt the skyline's belting beryl
    And the wine-dark flats below.

Royal the pageant closes,
    Lit by the last of the sun—
Opal and ash-of-roses,
    Cinnamon, umber, and dun.

BRIDGE-GUARD IN THE KARROO

The twilight swallows the thicket,
    The starlight reveals the ridge;
The whistle shrills to the picket
    We are changing guard on the bridge.

(Few, forgotten and lonely,
    Where the empty metals shine—
No, not combatants—only
    Details guarding the line.)

We slip through the broken panel
    Of fence by the ganger's shed;
We drop to the waterless channel
    And the lean track overhead;

We stumble on refuse of rations,
    The beef and the biscuit-tins;
We take our appointed stations,
    And the endless night begins.

We hear the Hottentot herders
    As the sheep click past to the fold—
And the click of the restless girders
    As the steel contracts in the cold—

BRIDGE-GUARD IN THE KARROO

Voices of jackals calling
  And, loud in the hush between,
A morsel of dry earth falling
  From the flanks of the scarred ravine.

And the solemn firmament marches,
  And the hosts of heaven rise
Framed through the iron arches—
  Banded and barred by the ties,

Till we feel the far track humming,
  And we see her headlight plain,
And we gather and wait her coming—
  The wonderful north-bound train.

(Few, forgotten and lonely,
  Where the white car-windows shine—
No, not combatants—only
  Details guarding the line.)

Quick, ere the gift escape us!
  Out of the darkness we reach
For a handful of week-old papers
  And a mouthful of human speech.

BRIDGE-GUARD IN THE KARROO

And the monstrous heaven rejoices,
    And the earth allows again
Meetings, greetings, and voices
    Of women talking with men.

So we return to our places,
    As out on the bridge she rolls;
And the darkness covers our faces,
    And the darkness re-enters our souls.

More than a little lonely
    Where the lessening tail-lights shine.
No—not combatants—only
    Details guarding the line!

THE LESSON

(1899–1902)

Let us admit it fairly, as a business people should,
We have had no end of a lesson : it will do us no end
  of good.

Not on a single issue, or in one direction or twain,
But conclusively, comprehensively, and several times
    and again,
Were all our most holy illusions knocked higher than
    Gilderoy's kite.
We have had a jolly good lesson, and it serves us
    jolly well right!

This was not bestowed us under the trees, nor yet in
    the shade of a tent,
But swingingly, over eleven degrees of a bare brown
    continent.

THE LESSON

From Lamberts to Delagoa Bay, and from Pieters-
    burg to Sutherland,
Fell the phenomenal lesson we learned—with a full-
    ness accorded no other land.

It was our fault, and our very great fault, and *not*
    the judgment of Heaven.
We made an Army in our own image, on an island
    nine by seven,
Which faithfully mirrored its makers' ideals, equip-
    ment, and mental attitude—
And so we got our lesson: and we ought to accept
    it with gratitude.

We have spent two hundred million pounds to prove
    the fact once more,
That horses are quicker than men afoot, since two
    and two make four:
And horses have four legs, and men have two legs,
    and two into four goes twice,
And nothing over except our lesson—and very cheap
    at the price.

For remember (this our children shall know: we are
    too near for that knowledge)
Not our mere astonied camps, but Council and Creed
    and College—

THE LESSON

All the obese, unchallenged old things that stifle and
    overlie us—
Have felt the effects of the lesson we got—an
    advantage no money could buy us!

Then let us develop this marvellous asset which we
    alone command,
And which, it may subsequently transpire, will be
    worth as much as the Rand:
Let us approach this pivotal fact in a humble yet
    hopeful mood—
We have had no end of a lesson: it will do us no
    end of good!

It was our fault, and our very great fault—and now
    we must turn it to use;
We have forty million reasons for failure, but not a
    single excuse!
So the more we work and the less we talk the better
    results we shall get—
We have had an Imperial lesson; it may make us an
    Empire yet!

THE FILES

FILES—
The Files—
Office Files!
Oblige me by referring to the files.
Every question man can raise,
Every phrase of every phase
Of that question is on record in the files—
(Threshed out threadbare—fought and finished in the
    files).
Ere the Universe at large
Was our new-tipped arrows' targe—
Ere we rediscovered Mammon and his wiles—
Faenza, gentle reader, spent her—five-and-twentieth
    leader
(You will find him, and some others, in the files).
Warn all future Robert Brownings and Carlyles,
It will interest them to hunt among the files,

116

THE FILES

Where unvisited, a-cold,
Lie the crowded years of old
In that Kensal-Green of greatness called the files—
(In our newspaPère-la-Chaise the office files),
Where the dead men lay them down
Meekly sure of long renown,
And above them, sere and swift,
Packs the daily deepening drift
Of the all-recording, all-effacing files—
The obliterating, automatic files.

Count the mighty men who slung
Ink, Evangel, Sword, or Tongue
When Reform and you were young—
Made their boasts and spake according in the files—
(Hear the ghosts that wake applauding in the files!)
Trace each all-forgot career
From long primer through brevier
Unto Death, a para minion in the files
(Para minion—solid—bottom of the files) . . . .

Some successful Kings and Queens adorn the files,
They were great, their views were leaded,
And their deaths were triple-headed,
So they catch the eye in running through the files
(Show as blazes in the mazes of the files);
For their " paramours and priests,"
And their gross, jack-booted feasts,
And their epoch-marking actions see the files.

THE FILES

Was it Bomba fled the blue Sicilian isles?
Was it Saffi a professor
Once of Oxford, wrought redress or
Garibaldi?—Who remembers
Forty-odd-year old Septembers?—
Only sextons paid to dig among the files
(Such as I am, born and bred among the files).
You must hack through much deposit
Ere you know for sure who was it
Came to burial with such honour in the files
(Only seven seasons back beneath the files).
" Very great our loss and grievous—
" So our best and brightest leave us,
" And it ends the Age of Giants," say the files;
All the '60—'70—'80—'90 files
(The open-minded, opportunist files—
The easy " O King, live for ever " files).
It is good to read a little in the files;
'Tis a sure and sovereign balm
Unto philosophic calm,
Yea, and philosophic doubt when Life beguiles.
When you know Success is Greatness,
When you marvel at your lateness
In apprehending facts so plain to Smiles
(Self-helpful, wholly strenuous Samuel Smiles),
When your Imp of Blind Desire
Bids you set the Thames afire,

THE FILES

You'll remember men have done so—in the files.
You'll have seen those flames transpire—in the files
(More than once that flood has run so—in the files).
When the Conchimarian horns
Of the reboantic Norns
Usher gentlemen and ladies
With new lights on Heaven and Hades,
Guaranteeing to Eternity
All yesterday's modernity;
When Brocken-spectres made by
Some one's breath on ink parade by,
Very earnest and tremendous,
Let not shows of shows offend us.
When of everything we like we
Shout ecstatic:—" *Quod ubique,*
Quod ab omnibus means *semper !* "
Oh, my brother, keep your temper!
Light your pipe and take a look along the files!
You've a better chance to guess
At the meaning of Success
(Which is Greatness—*vide* press)
When you've seen it in perspective in the files.

THE REFORMER

Not in the camp his victory lies
Or triumph in the market-place,
Who is his Nation's sacrifice
To turn the judgment from his race.

Happy is he who, bred and taught
    By sleek, sufficing Circumstance—
Whose Gospel was the apparelled thought,
    Whose Gods were Luxury and Chance—

Sees, on the threshold of his days,
    The old life shrivel like a scroll,
And to unheralded dismays
    Submits his body and his soul;

The fatted shows wherein he stood
    Foregoing, and the idiot pride,
That he may prove with his own blood
    All that his easy sires denied—

THE REFORMER

Ultimate issues, primal springs,
   Demands, abasements, penalties—
The imperishable plinth of things
   Seen and unseen, that touch our peace.

For, though ensnaring ritual dim
   His vision through the after-years,
Yet virtue shall go out of him:
   Example profiting his peers.

With great things charged he shall not hold
   Aloof till great occasion rise,
But serve, full-harnessed, as of old
   The days that are the destinies.

He shall forswear and put away
   The idols of his sheltered house;
And to Necessity shall pay
   Unflinching tribute of his vows.

He shall not plead another's act,
   Nor bind him in another's oath
To weigh the Word above the Fact,
   Or make or take excuse for sloth.

THE REFORMER

The yoke he bore shall press him still,
  And long-ingrained effort goad
To find, to fashion, and fulfil
  The cleaner life, the sterner code.

Not in the camp his victory lies—
  The world (unheeding his return)
Shall see it in his children's eyes
  And from his grandson's lips shall learn!

DIRGE OF DEAD SISTERS

WHO recalls the twilight and the ranged tents in
   order
   (Violet peaks uplifted through the crystal evening
   air?)
And the clink of iron teacups and the piteous, noble
   laughter,
   And the faces of the Sisters with the dust upon
   their hair?

(Now and not hereafter, while the breath is in our
   nostrils,
   Now and not hereafter, ere the meaner years go
   by—
Let us now remember many honourable women,
   Such as bade us turn again when we were like to
   die.)

Who recalls the morning and the thunder through
   the foothills,
   (Tufts of fleecy shrapnel strung along the empty
   plains?)

DIRGE OF DEAD SISTERS

And the sun-scarred Red-Cross coaches creeping
    guarded to the culvert,
  And the faces of the Sisters looking gravely from
    the trains?

(When the days were torment and the nights were
    clouded terror,
  When the Powers of Darkness had dominion on
    our souls—
When we fled consuming through the Seven Hells of
    fever,
  These put out their hands to us and healed and
    made us whole.)

Who recalls the midnight by the bridge's wrecked
    abutment
  (Autumn rain that rattled like a Maxim on the
    tin?)
And the lightning-dazzled levels and the streaming,
    straining wagons,
  And the faces of the Sisters as they bore the
    wounded in?

(Till the pain was merciful and stunned us into
    silence—
  When each nerve cried out on God that made the
    misused clay;

DIRGE OF DEAD SISTERS

When the Body triumphed and the last poor shame
    departed—
  These abode our agonies and wiped the sweat
    away.)

Who recalls the noontide and the funerals through
    the market
  (Blanket-hidden bodies, flagless, followed by the
    flies?)
And the footsore firing-party, and the dust and
    stench and staleness,
  And the faces of the Sisters and the glory in their
    eyes?

(Bold behind the battle, in the open camp
    all-hallowed,
  Patient, wise, and mirthful in the ringed and
    reeking town,
These endured unresting till they rested from their
    labours—
  Little wasted bodies, ah, so light to lower down!)

Yet their graves are scattered and their names are
    clean forgotten,
  Earth shall not remember, but the Waiting Angel
    knows

DIRGE OF DEAD SISTERS

Them that died at Uitvlugt when the plague was on
    the city—
    Her that fell at Simon's Town in service on our
    foes.

*Wherefore we they ransomed, while the breath is in
    our nostrils,
    Now and not hereafter, ere the meaner years go
    by—
Praise with love and worship many honourable
    women,
    Those that gave their lives for us when we were
    like to die!*

THE ISLANDERS

*No doubt but ye are the People—your throne is above
    the King's.*
*Whoso speaks in your presence must say acceptable
    things :*
*Bowing the head in worship, bending the knee in
    fear—*
*Bringing the word well smoothen—such as a King
    should hear.*

Fenced by your careful fathers, ringed by your
    leaden seas,
Long did ye wake in quiet and long lie down at
    ease ;
Till ye said of Strife, " What is it? " of the Sword,
    "It is far from our ken ";
Till ye made a sport of your shrunken hosts and a
    toy of your armed men.

127

THE ISLANDERS

Ye stopped your ears to the warning—ye would
neither look nor heed—

Ye set your leisure before their toil and your lusts
above their need.

Because of your witless learning and your beasts of
warren and chase,

Ye grudged your sons to their service and your fields
for their camping-place.

Ye forced them glean in the highways the straw for
the bricks they brought;

Ye forced them follow in byways the craft that ye
never taught.

Ye hindered and hampered and crippled; ye thrust
out of sight and away

Those that would serve you for honour and those
that served you for pay.

Then were the judgments loosened; then was your
shame revealed,

At the hands of a little people, few but apt in the field.

Yet ye were saved by a remnant (and your land's
long-suffering Star),

When your strong men cheered in their millions
while your striplings went to the war.

Sons of the sheltered city—unmade, unhandled,
unmeet—

Ye pushed them raw to the battle as ye picked them
raw from the street.

And what did ye look they should compass? War-
craft learned in a breath,

Knowledge unto occasion at the first far view of
Death?

So! And ye train your horses and the dogs ye feed
and prize?

How are the beasts more worthy than the souls your
sacrifice?

But ye said, "Their valour shall show them"; but
ye said, "The end is close."

And ye sent them comfits and pictures to help them
harry your foes,

And ye vaunted your fathomless power, and ye
flaunted your iron pride,

Ere—ye fawned on the Younger Nations for the men
who could shoot and ride!

Then ye returned to your trinkets; then ye contented
your souls

With the flannelled fools at the wicket or the muddied
oafs at the goals.

Given to strong delusion, wholly believing a lie,

Ye saw that the land lay fenceless, and ye let the
months go by

Waiting some easy wonder: hoping some saving
sign—

Idle—openly idle—in the lee of the forespent
Line.

THE ISLANDERS

Idle—except for your boasting—and what is your
    boasting worth
If ye grudge a year of service to the lordliest life on
    earth?
Ancient, effortless, ordered, cycle on cycle set,
Life so long untroubled, that ye who inherit forget
It was not made with the mountains, it is not one
    with the deep.
Men, not gods, devised it.   Men, not gods, must
    keep.
Men, not children, servants or kinsfolk called from afar,
But each man born in the Island broke to the matter
    of war.
Soberly and by custom taken and trained for the
    same;
Each man born in the Island entered at youth to the
    game—
As it were almost cricket, not to be mastered in haste,
But after trial and labour, by temperance, living
    chaste.
As it were almost cricket—as it were even your play,
Weighed and pondered and worshipped, and
    practised day and day.
So ye shall bide sure-guarded when the restless
    lightnings wake
In the womb of the blotting war-cloud, and the
    pallid nations quake.

THE ISLANDERS

So, at the haggard trumpets, instant your soul shall
    leap
Forthright, accoutred, accepting—alert from the
    wells of sleep.
So at the threat ye shall summon—so at the need ye
    shall send
Men, not children or servants, tempered and taught
    to the end;
Cleansed of servile panic, slow to dread or despise,
Humble because of knowledge, mighty by
    sacrifice.
But ye say, " It will mar our comfort."   Ye say, "It
    will minish our trade."
Do ye wait for the spattered shrapnel ere ye learn
    how a gun is laid?
For the low, red glare to southward when the raided
    coast-towns burn?
(Light ye shall have on that lesson, but little time to
    learn.)
Will ye pitch some white pavilion, and lustily even
    the odds,
With nets and hoops and mallets, with rackets and
    bats and rods?
Will the rabbit war with your foemen—the red deer
    horn them for hire?
Your kept cock-pheasant keep you?—he is master of
    many a shire.

THE ISLANDERS

Arid, aloof, incurious, unthinking, unthanking,
    gelt,
Will ye loose your schools to flout them till their
    browbeat columns melt?
Will ye pray them or preach them, or print them, or
    ballot them back from your shore?
Will your workmen issue a mandate to bid them
    strike no more?
Will ye rise and dethrone your rulers? (Because ye
    were idle both?
Pride by insolence chastened? Indolence purged by
    sloth?)
No doubt but ye are the People; who shall make
    you afraid?
Also your gods are many; no doubt but your gods
    shall aid.
Idols of greasy altars built for the body's
    ease;
Proud little brazen Baals and talking fetishes;
Teraphs of sept and party and wise wood-pavement
    gods—
These shall come down to the battle and snatch you
    from under the rods?
From the gusty, flickering gun-roll with viewless
    salvoes rent,
And the pitted hail of the bullets that tell not whence
    they were sent.

THE ISLANDERS

When ye are ringed as with iron, when ye are
    scourged as with whips,
When the meat is yet in your belly, and the boast is
    yet on your lips;
When ye go forth at morning and the noon beholds
    you broke,
Ere ye lie down at even, your remnant, under the
    yoke.

*No doubt but ye are the People—absolute, strong, and
    wise;*
*Whatever your heart has desired ye have not withheld
    from your eyes.*
*On your own heads, in your own hands, the sin and
    the saving lies!*

THE PEACE OF DIVES

THE Word came down to Dives in Torment where
    he lay:
" Our World is full of wickedness, My Children maim
    and slay,
  " And the Saint and Seer and Prophet
  " Can make no better of it
" Than to sanctify and prophesy and pray.

" Rise up, rise up, thou Dives, and take again thy
    gold,
" And thy women and thy housen as they were to
    thee of old.
  " It may be grace hath found thee
  " In the furnace where We bound thee,
" And that thou shalt bring the peace My Son
    foretold."

THE PEACE OF DIVES

Then merrily rose Dives and leaped from out his fire,
And walked abroad with diligence to do the Lord's
     desire;
  And anon the battle ceased,
  And the captives were released,
And Earth had rest from Goshen to Gadire.

The Word came down to Satan that raged and
     roared alone,
Mid the shouting of the peoples by the cannon
     overthrown
  (But the Prophets, Saints, and Seers
  Set each other by the ears,
For each would claim the marvel as his own):

" Rise up, rise up, thou Satan, upon the Earth to go,
" And prove the peace of Dives if it be good or no:
  " For all that he hath planned
  " We deliver to thy hand,
" As thy skill shall serve to break it or bring low."

Then mightily rose Satan, and about the Earth he hied,
And breathed on Kings in idleness and Princes drunk
     with pride;
  But for all the wrong he breathed
  There was never sword unsheathed,
And the fires he lighted flickered out and died.

THE PEACE OF DIVES

Then terribly rose Satan, and he darkened Earth afar,
Till he came on cunning Dives where the money-
        changers are;
    And he saw men pledge their gear
    For the gold that buys the spear,
And the helmet and the habergeon of war.

Yea to Dives came the Persian and the Syrian and
        the Mede—
And their hearts were nothing altered, nor their
        cunning nor their greed—
    And they pledged their flocks and farms
    For the king-compelling arms,
And Dives lent according to their need.

Then Satan said to Dives:—" Return again with me,
" Who hast broken His Commandment in the day
        He set thee free,
    " Who grindest for thy greed,
    " Man's belly-pinch and need;
" And the blood of Man to filthy usury!"

Then softly answered Dives where the money-
        changers sit:—
" My refuge is Our Master, O My Master in the Pit;
    " But behold all Earth is laid
    " In the peace which I have made,
" And behold I wait on thee to trouble it!"

THE PEACE OF DIVES

Then angrily turned Satan, and about the Seas he
    fled,
To shake the new-sown peoples with insult, doubt,
    and dread;
  But for all the sleight he used
  There was never squadron loosed,
And the brands he flung flew dying and fell dead.

Yet to Dives came Atlantis and the Captains of the
    West—
And their hates were nothing weakened nor their
    anger nor unrest—
  And they pawned their utmost trade
  For the dry, decreeing blade;
And Dives lent and took of them their best.

Then Satan said to Dives:—" Declare thou by The
    Name,
" The secret of thy subtlety that turneth mine to
    shame.
  " It is known through all the Hells
  " How my peoples mocked my spells,
" And my faithless Kings denied me ere I came."

Then answered cunning Dives:—" Do not gold and
    hate abide
" At the heart of every Magic, yea, and senseless
    fear beside?

THE PEACE OF DIVES

" With gold and fear and hate

" I have harnessed state to state,

" And with hate and fear and gold their hates are
   tied.

" For hate men seek a weapon, for fear they seek a
   shield—

" Keener blades and broader targes than their frantic
   neighbours wield—

" For gold I arm their hands,

" And for gold I buy their lands,

" And for gold I sell their enemies the yield.

" Their nearest foes may purchase, or their furthest
   friends may lease,

" One by one from Ancient Accad to the Islands of
   the Seas.

" And their covenants they make

" For the naked iron's sake,

" But I—I trap them armoured into peace.

" The flocks that Egypt pledged me to Assyria I
   drave,

" And Pharaoh hath the increase of the herds that
   Sargon gave.

" Not for Ashdod overthrown

" Will the Kings destroy their own,

" Or their peoples wake the strife they feign to brave.

THE PEACE OF DIVES

"Is not Calno like Carchemish? For the steeds of
    their desire
"They have sold me seven harvests that I sell to
    Crowning Tyre;
  "And the Tyrian sweeps the plains
  "With a thousand hired wains,
"And the Cities keep the peace and—share the hire.

"Hast thou seen the pride of Moab? For the
    swords about his path,
"His bond is to Philistia, in half of all he hath;
  "And he dare not draw the sword
  "Till Gaza give the word,
"And he show release from Askalon and Gath.

"Wilt thou call again thy peoples, wilt thou craze
    anew thy Kings?
"Lo! my lightnings pass before thee, and their
    whistling servant brings,
  "Ere the drowsy street hath stirred—
  "Every masked and midnight word,
"And the nations break their fast upon these things.

"So I make a jest of Wonder, and a mock of Time
    and Space,
"The roofless Seas an hostel, and the Earth a market-
    place,

THE PEACE OF DIVES

" Where the anxious traders know

" Each is surety for his foe,

" And none may thrive without his fellows' grace.

" Now this is all my subtlety and this is all my wit,

" God give thee good enlightenment, My Master in
   the Pit.

   " But behold all Earth is laid

   " In the peace which I have made,

" And behold I wait on thee to trouble it!"

SOUTH AFRICA

LIVED a woman wonderful,
   (May the Lord amend her!)
Neither simple, kind, nor true,
But her Pagan beauty drew
Christian gentlemen a few
   Hotly to attend her.

Christian gentlemen a few
   From Berwick unto Dover ;
For she was South Africa,
And she was South Africa,
She was our South Africa,
   Africa all over !

Half her land was dead with drouth,
   Half was red with battle;
She was fenced with fire and sword,
Plague on pestilence outpoured,
Locusts on the greening sward
   And murrain on the cattle!

141

SOUTH AFRICA

True, ah true, and overtrue ;
That is why we love her !
For she is South Africa,
And she is South Africa,
She is our South Africa,
Africa all over !

Bitter hard her lovers toiled,
 Scandalous their payment,—
Food forgot on trains derailed ;
Cattle-dung where fuel failed ;
Water where the mules had staled ;
 And sackcloth for their raiment !

So she filled their mouths with dust
 And their bones with fever ;
Greeted them with cruel lies ;
Treated them despiteful-wise ;
Meted them calamities
 Till they vowed to leave her.

They took ship and they took sail,
 Raging, from her borders,—
In a little, none the less,
They forgat their sore duresse,
They forgave her waywardness
 And returned for orders !

SOUTH AFRICA

They esteemed her favour more
   Than a Throne's foundation.
For the glory of her face
Bade farewell to breed and race—
Yea, and made their burial-place
   Altar of a Nation!

Wherefore, being bought by blood
   And by blood restorèd
To the arms that nearly lost,
She, because of all she cost,
Stands, a very woman, most
   Perfect and adorèd!

On your feet, and let them know
   This is why we love her!
For she is South Africa,
She is our South Africa,
Is our own South Africa,
   Africa all over!

THE SETTLER

HERE, where my fresh-turned furrows run,
  And the deep soil glistens red,
I will repair the wrong that was done
  To the living and the dead.
Here, where the senseless bullet fell,
  And the barren shrapnel burst,
I will plant a tree, I will dig a well,
  Against the heat and the thirst.

Here, in a large and a sunlit land,
  Where no wrong bites to the bone,
I will lay my hand in my neighbour's hand,
  And together we will atone
For the set folly and the red breach
  And the black waste of it all,
Giving and taking counsel each
  Over the cattle-kraal.

144

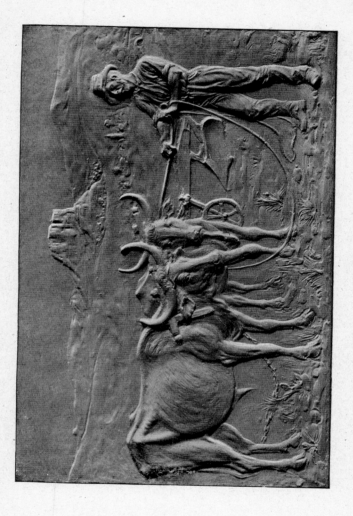

THE SETTLER

Here will we join against our foes—
  The hailstroke and the storm,
And the red and rustling cloud that blows
  The locust's mile-deep swarm;
Frost and murrain and floods let loose
  Shall launch us side by side
In the holy wars that have no truce
  'Twixt seed and harvest-tide.

Earth, where we rode to slay or be slain,
  Our love shall redeem unto life;
We will gather and lead to her lips again
  The waters of ancient strife,
From the far and fiercely guarded streams
  And the pools where we lay in wait,
Till the corn cover our evil dreams
  And the young corn our hate.

And when we bring old fights to mind,
  We will not remember the sin—
If there be blood on his head of my kind
  Or blood on my head of his kin—
For the ungrazed upland, the untilled lea
  Cry, and the fields forlorn:
"The dead must bury their dead, but ye—
  Ye serve an host unborn."

145

THE SETTLER

Bless then, our God, the new-yoked plough
  And the good beasts that draw,
And the bread we eat in the sweat of our brow
  According to Thy Law.
After us cometh a multitude—
  Prosper the work of our hands,
That we may feed with our land's food
  The folk of all our lands!

Here, in the waves and the troughs of the plains,
  Where the healing stillness lies,
And the vast, benignant sky restrains
  And the long days make wise—
Bless to our use the rain and the sun
  And the blind seed in its bed,
That we may repair the wrong that was done
  To the living and the dead!

SERVICE SONGS

" Tommy" you was when it began,
  But now that it is o'er
You shall be called The Service Man
  'Enceforward, evermore.

Batt'ry, brigade, flank, centre, van,
  Defaulter, Army corps—
From first to last The Service Man
  'Enceforward, evermore.

From 'Alifax to 'Industan,
  From York to Singapore—
'Orse, foot, an' guns, The Service Man
  'Enceforward, evermore !

CHANT—PAGAN

ENGLISH IRREGULAR : '99–'02

ME that 'ave been what I've been,
Me that 'ave gone where I've gone,
Me that 'ave seen what I've seen—
  'Ow can I ever take on
With awful old England again,
An' 'ouses both sides of the street,
And 'edges two sides of the lane,
And the parson an' "gentry" between,
An' touchin' my 'at when we meet—
  Me that 'ave been what I've been?

Me that 'ave watched 'arf a world
'Eave up all shiny with dew,
Kopje on kop to the sun,
An' as soon as the mist let 'em through

149

CHANT—PAGAN

Our 'elios winkin' like fun—
Three sides of a ninety-mile square,
Over valleys as big as a shire—
Are ye there?   Are ye there?   Are ye there?
An' then the blind drum of our fire . . .
An' I'm rollin' 'is lawns for the Squire,

           Me!

Me that 'ave rode through the dark
Forty mile often on end,
Along the Ma'ollisberg Range,
With only the stars for my mark
An' only the night for my friend,
An' things runnin' off as you pass,
An' things jumpin' up in the grass,
An' the silence, the shine an' the size
Of the 'igh, inexpressible skies. . . .
I am takin' some letters almost
As much as a mile, to the post,
An' "mind you come back with the change!"

           Me!

Me that saw Barberton took
When we dropped through the clouds on their 'ead,
An' they 'ove the guns over an' fled—
Me that was through Di'mond 'Ill,
An' Pieters an' Springs an' Belfast—

CHANT—PAGAN

From Dundee to Vereeniging all!
Me that stuck out to the last
(An' five bloomin' bars on my chest)—
I am doin' my Sunday-school best,
By the 'elp of the Squire an' 'is wife
(Not to mention the 'ousemaid an' cook),
To come in an' 'ands up an' be still,
An' honestly work for my bread,
My livin' in that state of life
To which it shall please God to call

                         Me!

Me that 'ave followed my trade
In the place where the lightnin's are made,
'Twixt the Rains and the Sun and the Moon;
Me that lay down an' got up
Three years an' the sky for my roof—
That 'ave ridden my 'unger an' thirst
Six thousand raw mile on the 'oof,
With the Vaal and the Orange for cup,
An' the Brandwater Basin for dish,—
Oh! it's 'ard to be'ave as they wish
(Too 'ard, an' a little too soon),
I'll 'ave to think over it first—

                         Me!

I will arise an' get 'ence;—
I will trek South and make sure

CHANT—PAGAN

If it's only my fancy or not
That the sunshine of England is pale,
And the breezes of England are stale,
An' there's somethin' gone small with the lot;
For *I* know of a sun an' a wind,
An' some plains and a mountain be'ind,
An' some graves by a barb-wire fence;
An' a Dutchman I've fought 'oo might give
Me a job were I ever inclined,
To look in an' offsaddle an' live
Where there's neither a road nor a tree—
But only my Maker an' me,
And I think it will kill me or cure,
So I think I will go there an' see.

M. I.

(MOUNTED INFANTRY OF THE LINE)

I WISH my mother could see me now, with a
    fence-post under my arm,
And a knife and a spoon in my putties that I found
    on a Boer farm,
Atop of a sore-backed Argentine, with a thirst that
    you couldn't buy.
  I used to be in the Yorkshires once
  (Sussex, Lincolns, and Rifles once),
   Hampshires, Glosters, and Scottish once! *(ad lib.)*
     But now I am M. I.

That is what we are known as—that is the name you
    must call
If you want officers' servants, pickets an' 'orse-guards
    an' all—

M. I.

Details for buryin'-parties, company-cooks or
supply—
Turn out the chronic Ikonas!   Roll up the ——— [1]
M. I.!

My 'ands are spotty with veldt-sores, my shirt is a
button an' frill,
An' the things I've used my bay'nit for would make
a tinker ill!
An' I don't know whose dam' column I'm in, nor
where we're trekkin' nor why.
I've trekked from the Vaal to the Orange once—
From the Vaal to the greasy Pongolo once—
(Or else it was called the Zambesi once)—
For now I am M. I.

That is what we are known as—we are the push you
require
For outposts all night under freezin', an' rear-guard
all day under fire.
Anything 'ot or unwholesome?   Anything dusty or
dry?
Borrow a bunch of Ikonas!   Trot out the ———
M. I.!

[1] Number according to taste and service of audience.

M. I.

Our Sergeant-Major's a subaltern, our Captain's a
    Fusilier—
Our Adjutant's "late of Somebody's 'Orse," an' a
    Melbourne auctioneer;
But you couldn't spot us at 'arf a mile from the
    crackest caval-ry.
  They used to talk about Lancers once,
  Hussars, Dragoons, an' Lancers once,
  'Elmets, pistols, an' carbines once,
        But now we are M. I.

That is what we are known as—we are the orphans
    they blame
For beggin' the loan of an 'ead-stall an' makin' a
    mount to the same:
'Can't even look at an 'orselines but some one goes
    bellerin' " Hi!
" 'Ere comes a burglin' Ikona!" Footsack you
    —— M. I.!

We're trekkin' our twenty miles a day an' bein'
    loved by the Dutch,
But we don't hold on by the mane no more, nor lose
    our stirrups—much;

155

M. I.

An' we scout with a senior man in charge where the
    'oly white flags fly.
  We used to think they were friendly once,
  Didn't take any precautions once
  (Once, my ducky, an' only once!)
        But now we are M. I.!

That is what we are known as—we are the beggars
    that got
Three days " to learn equitation," an' six months o'
    bloomin' well trot!
Cow-guns, an' cattle, an' convoys—an' Mister De
    Wet on the fly—
We are the rollin' Ikonas!   We are the —— M. I.!

The new fat regiments come from home, imaginin'
    vain V. C.'s
(The same as our talky-fighty men which are often
    Number Threes[1]),
But our words o' command are " Scatter " an'
    " Close " an' " Let your wounded lie."
  We used to rescue 'em noble once,—
  Givin' the range as we raised 'em once,
  Gettin' 'em killed as we saved 'em once—
        But now we are M. I.

[1] Horse-holders when in action, and therefore generally under cover.

M. I.

That is what we are known as—we are the lanterns
    you view
After a fight round the kopjes, lookin' for men that
    we knew;
Whistlin' an' callin' together, 'altin' to catch the
    reply: —
" 'Elp me! O 'elp me, Ikonas!" This way, the ——
    M. I.!

I wish my mother could see me now, a-gatherin'
    news on my own,
When I ride like a General up to the scrub and ride
    back like Tod Sloan,
Remarkable close to my 'orse's neck to let the shots
    go by.
  We used to fancy it risky once
  (Called it a reconnaissance once),
  Under the charge of an orf'cer once,
        But now we are M. I.

That is what we are known as—that is the song you
    must say
When you want men to be Mausered at one and a
    penny a day;

M. I.

We are no five-bob colonials—we are the 'ome-made
  supply,
Ask for the London Ikonas!   Ring up the ——
  M. I.!

I wish myself could talk to myself as I left 'im a year
  ago;
I could tell 'im a lot that would save 'im a lot on the
  things that 'e ought to know!
When I think o' that ignorant barrack-bird, it almost
  makes me cry.
  I· used to belong in an Army once
  (Gawd! what a rum little Army once),
  Red little, dead little Army once!
        But now I am M. I.!

That is what we are known as—we are the men that
  have been
Over a year at the business, smelt it an' felt it an'
  seen.
We 'ave got 'old of the needful—*you* will be told by
  and bye;
Wait till you've 'eard the Ikonas, spoke to the old
  M. I.!

M. I.

Mount—march, Ikonas! Stand to your 'orses again!
Mop off the frost on the saddles, mop up the miles on
*   the plain.*
Out go the stars in the dawnin', up goes our dust to
*   the sky,*
Walk—trot, Ikonas! Trek jou,[1] *the old M. I.!*

[1] Get ahead.

COLUMNS

(MOBILE COLUMNS OF THE LATER WAR)

OUT o' the wilderness, dusty an' dry
    (Time, an' 'igh time to be trekkin' again!)
'Oo is it 'eads to the Detail Supply?
    (A section, a pompom, an' six 'undred men).

'Ere comes the clerk with 'is lantern an' keys
    (Time, an' 'igh time to be trekkin' again!)
" Surplus of everything—draw what you please
    " For the section, the pompom, an' six 'undred men."

" What are our orders an' where do we lay? "
    (Time, an' 'igh time to be trekkin' again!)
" You came after dark—you will leave before day,
    *" You section, you pompom, an' six 'undred men!" *

COLUMNS

Down the tin street, 'alf awake an' unfed,
'Ark to 'em blessin' the Gen'ral in bed!

Now by the church an' the outspan they wind—
Over the ridge an' it's all lef' be'ind
   For the section, etc.

Soon they will camp as the dawn 's growin' grey,
Roll up for coffee an' sleep while they may—
   The section, etc.

Read their 'ome letters, their papers an' such,
For they'll move after dark to astonish the Dutch
   With a section, etc.

'Untin' for shade as the long hours pass,
Blankets on rifles or burrows in grass,
   Lies the section, etc.

Dossin' or beatin' a shirt in the sun,
Watchin' chameleons or cleanin' a gun,
   Waits the section, etc.

With nothin' but stillness as far as you please,
An' the silly mirage stringin' islands an' seas
   Round the section, etc.

COLUMNS

So they strips off their hide an' they grills in their
    bones,
Till the shadows crawl out from beneath the pore
    stones
    Towards the section, etc.

An' the Mauser-bird stops an' the jackals begin,
An' the 'orse-guard comes up an' the Gunners 'ook
    in
    As a 'int to the pompom an' six 'undred
    men. . . .

Off through the dark with the stars to rely on—
(Alpha Centauri an' somethin' Orion)
    Moves the section, etc.

Same bloomin' 'ole which the ant-bear 'as broke,
Same bloomin' stumble an' same bloomin' joke
    Down the section, etc.

Same " which is right?" where the cart-tracks
    divide,
Same " give it up" from the same clever guide
    To the section, etc.

COLUMNS

Same tumble-down on the same 'idden farm,
Same white-eyed Kaffir 'oo gives the alarm
  Of the section, etc.

Same shootin' wild at the end o' the night,
Same flyin' tackle an' same messy fight
  By the section, etc.

Same ugly 'iccup an' same 'orrid squeal,
When it's too dark to see an' it's too late to feel
  In the section, etc.

(Same batch of prisoners, 'airy an' still,
Watchin' their comrades bolt over the 'ill
  From the section, etc.)

Same chilly glare in the eye of the sun
As 'e gets up displeasured to see what was done
  By the section, etc.

Same splash o' pink on the stoep or the kraal,
An' the same quiet face which 'as finished with all
  In the section, the pompom, an' six 'undred men.

COLUMNS

Out o' the wilderness, dusty an' dry
  (Time, an' 'igh time to be trekkin' again!)
'Oo is it 'eads to the Detail Supply?
  (A section, a pompom, an' six 'undred men).

THE PARTING OF THE COLUMNS

" . . . On the —th instant a mixed detachment of colonials
left —— for Cape Town, there to rejoin their respective home-
ward-bound contingents, after fifteen months' service in the
field. They were escorted to the station by the regular
troops in garrison and the bulk of Colonel ——'s column, which
has just come in to refit, preparatory to further operations.
The leave-taking was of the most cordial character, the men
cheering each other continuously."—*Any Newspaper.*

WE'VE rode and fought and ate and drunk as rations
    come to hand,
Together for a year and more around this stinkin'
    land :
Now you are goin' home again, but we must see it
    through,
We needn't tell we liked you well. Good-bye—
    good luck to you!

THE PARTING OF THE COLUMNS

You 'ad no special call to come, and so you doubled
    out,

And learned us how to camp and cook an' steal a
    horse and scout:

Whatever game we fancied most, you joyful played
    it too,

And rather better on the whole.   Good-bye—good
    luck to you!

There isn't much we 'aven't shared, since Kruger
    cut an' run,

The same old work, the same old skoff, the same old
    dust and sun;

The same old chance that laid us out, or winked an'
    let us through;

The same old Life, the same old Death. Good-bye—
    good luck to you!

Our blood 'as truly mixed with yours—all down the
    Red Cross train,

We've bit the same thermometer in Bloeming-
    typhoidtein.

We've 'ad the same old temp'rature—the same
    relapses too,

The same old saw-backed fever-chart. Good-bye—
    good luck to you!

THE PARTING OF THE COLUMNS

But 'twasn't merely this an' that (which all the world
    may know),
'Twas how you talked an' looked at things which
    made us like you so.
All independent, queer an' odd, but most amazin'
    new,
My word! you shook us up to rights.   Good-bye—
    good luck to you!

Think o' the stories round the fire, the tales along
    the trek—
O' Calgary an' Wellin'ton, an' Sydney and Quebec;
Of mine an' farm, an' ranch an' run, an' moose an'
    cariboo,
An' parrots peckin' lambs to death!   Good-bye—
    good luck to you!

We've seen you 'ome by word o' mouth, we've
    watched your rivers shine,
We've 'eard your bloomin' forests blow of eucalip'
    an' pine;
Your young, gay countries north an' south, we feel
    we own 'em too,
For they was made by rank an' file.   Good-bye—
    good luck to you!

THE PARTING OF THE COLUMNS

We'll never read the papers now without inquirin'
    first
For word from all those friendly dorps where you
    was born an' nursed.
Why, Dawson, Galle, an' Montreal—Port Darwin—
    Timaru,
They're only just across the road!   Good-bye—
    good luck to you!

Good-bye!—So long! Don't lose yourselves—nor
    us, nor all kind friends,
But tell the girls your side the drift we're comin'—
    when it ends!
Good-bye, you bloomin' Atlases! You've taught us
    somethin' new:
The world's no bigger than a kraal. Good-bye—
    good luck to you!

TWO KOPJES

(MADE YEOMANRY)

ONLY two African kopjes,
   Only the cart-tracks that wind
Empty and open between 'em,
   Only the Transvaal behind:
Only an Aldershot column
   Marching to conquer the land . . .
Only a sudden and solemn
   Visit, unarmed, to the Rand.

   Then scorn not the African kopje,
      The kopje that smiles in the heat,
   The wholly unoccupied kopje,
      The home of Cornelius and Piet.
   You can never be sure of your kopje,
      But of this be you blooming well sure,
   A kopje is always a kopje,
      And a Boojer is always a Boer!

TWO KOPJES

Only two African kopjes,
   Only the vultures above,
Only baboons—at the bottom,
   Only some buck on the move;
Only a Kensington draper
   Only pretendin' to scout . . .
Only bad news for the paper,
   Only another knock-out.

   Then mock not the African kopje,
     And rub not your flank on its side,
   The silent and simmering kopje,
     The kopje beloved by the guide.
   You can never be, etc.

Only two African kopjes,
   Only the dust of their wheels,
Only a bolted commando,
   Only our guns at their heels . . .
Only a little barb-wire,
   Only a natural fort,
Only " by sections retire,"
   Only " regret to report "!

TWO KOPJES

Then mock not the African kopje,
   Especially when it is twins,
One sharp and one table-topped kopje,
   For that's where the trouble begins.
  You can never be, etc.

Only two African kopjes
   Baited the same as before—
Only we've had it so often,
   Only we're taking no more . . .
Only a wave to our troopers,
   Only our flanks swinging past,
Only a dozen voorloopers,
   Only *we*'ve learned it at last!

Then mock not the African kopje,
   But take off your hat to the same,
The patient, impartial old kopje,
   The kopje that taught us the game!
For all that we knew in the Columns,
   And all they've forgot on the Staff,
We learned at the fight o' Two Kopjes,
   Which lasted two years an' a half.

171

TWO KOPJES

O mock not the African kopje,
Not even when peace has been signed—
The kopje that isn't a kopje—
The kopje that copies its kind.
You can never be sure of your kopje,
But of this be you blooming well sure,
That a kopje is always a kopje,
And a Boojer is always a Boer!

THE INSTRUCTOR

(CORPORALS)

AT times when under cover I 'ave said,
To keep my spirits up an' raise a laugh,
'Earin' 'im pass so busy over-'ead—
Old Nickel Neck, 'oo isn't on the Staff—
"There's one above is greater than us all."

Before 'im I 'ave seen my Colonel fall,
An' watched 'im write my Captain's epitaph,
So that a long way off it could be read—
He *'as* the knack o' makin' men feel small—
Old Whistle Tip, 'oo isn't on the Staff.

There is no sense in fleein' (I 'ave fled),
Better go on an' do the belly-crawl,
An' 'ope 'e'll 'it some other man instead
Of you 'e seems to 'unt so speshual—
Fitzy van Spitz, 'oo isn't on the Staff.

173

THE INSTRUCTOR

An' thus in mem'ry's gratis biograph,
Now that the show is over, I recall
The peevish voice an' 'oary mushroom 'ead
Of 'im we owned was greater than us all,
'Oo give instruction to the quick an' the dead—
The Shudderin' Beggar not upon the Staff.

BOOTS

(INFANTRY COLUMNS OF THE EARLIER WAR)

WE'RE foot—slog—slog—slog—sloggin' over
    Africa!
Foot—foot—foot—foot—sloggin' over Africa—
(Boots—boots—boots—boots, movin' up an' down
    again!)
            There's no discharge in the war!

Seven—six—eleven—five—nine-an'-twenty mile
    to-day—
Four—eleven—seventeen—thirty-two the day
    before—
(Boots—boots—boots—boots, movin' up an' down
    again!)
            There's no discharge in the war!

175

BOOTS

Don't—don't—don't—don't—look at what's in front
of you
(Boots—boots—boots—boots, movin' up an' down
again);
Men—men—men—men—men go mad with watchin'
'em,
    An' there's no discharge in the war!

Try—try—try—try—to think o' something
different—
Oh—my—God—keep—me from goin' lunatic!
(Boots—boots—boots—boots, movin' up an' down
again!)
    There's no discharge in the war!

Count—count—count—count—the bullets in the
bandoliers;
If—your—eyes—drop—they will get atop o' you
(Boots—boots—boots—boots, movin' up an' down
again)—
    There's no discharge in the war!

We—can—stick—out—'unger, thirst, an' weariness,
But—not—not—not—not the chronic sight of 'em—
Boots—boots—boots—boots, movin' up an' down
again,
    An' there's no discharge in the war!

BOOTS

'Tain't—so—bad—by—day because o' company,
But night—brings—long—strings o' forty thousand
    million
Boots—boots—boots—boots, movin' up an' down
    again.
             There's no discharge in the war!

I—'ave—marched—six—weeks in 'Ell an' certify
It—is—not—fire—devils dark or anything
But boots—boots—boots, movin' up an' down again,
        An' there's no discharge in the war!

THE MARRIED MAN

(RESERVIST OF THE LINE)

THE bachelor 'e fights for one
    As joyful as can be;
But the married man don't call it fun,
    Because 'e fights for three—
For 'Im an' 'Er an' It
    (An' Two an' One makes Three)
'E wants to finish 'is little bit,
    An' 'e wants to go 'ome to 'is tea!

The bachelor pokes up 'is head
    To see if you are gone;
But the married man lies down instead,
    An' waits till the sights come on.
For 'Im an' 'Er an' a hit
    (Direct or ricochee)
'E wants to finish 'is little bit,
    An' 'e wants to go 'ome to 'is tea.

178

THE MARRIED MAN

The bachelor will miss you clear
　　To fight another day;
But the married man, 'e says " No fear!"
　　'E wants you out of the way
Of 'Im an' 'Er an' It
　　(An' 'is road to 'is farm or the sea),
'E wants to finish 'is little bit,
　　An' 'e wants to go 'ome to 'is tea.

The bachelor 'e fights 'is fight
　　An' stretches out an' snores;
But the married man sits up all night—
　　For 'e don't like out o' doors:
'E'll strain an' listen an' peer
　　An' give the first alarm—
For the sake o' the breathin' 'e's used to 'ear
　　An' the 'ead on the thick of 'is arm.

The bachelor may risk 'is 'ide
　　To 'elp you when you're downed;
But the married man will wait beside
　　Till the ambulance comes round.
'E'll take your 'ome address
　　An' all you've time to say,
Or if 'e sees there's 'ope, 'e'll press
　　Your art'ry 'alf the day—

THE MARRIED MAN

For 'Im an' 'Er an' It
   (An' One from Three leaves Two),
For 'e knows you wanted to finish your bit,
   An' 'e knows 'oo's wantin' you.
Yes, 'Im an' 'Er an' It
   (Our 'oly One in Three),
We're all of us anxious to finish our bit,
   An' we want to get 'ome to our tea!

Yes, It an' 'Er an' 'Im,
   Which often makes me think
The married man must sink or swim
   An'—'e can't afford to sink!
Oh 'Im an' It an' 'Er
   Since Adam an' Eve began,
So I'd rather fight with the bacheler
   An' be nursed by the married man!

LICHTENBERG

(N. S. W. CONTINGENT)

SMELLS are surer than sounds or sights
  To make your heart-strings crack—
They start those awful voices o' nights
  That whisper, " Old man, come back."
That must be why the big things pass
  And the little things remain,
Like the smell of the wattle by Lichtenberg,
  Riding in, in the rain.

There was some silly fire on the flank
  And the small wet drizzling down—
There were the sold-out shops and the bank
  And the wet, wide-open town;
And we were doing escort-duty
  To somebody's baggage-train,
And I smelt wattle by Lichtenberg—
  Riding in, in the rain.

LICHTENBERG

It was all Australia to me—
   All I had found or missed:
Every face I was crazy to see,
   And every woman I'd kissed:
All that I shouldn't ha' done, God knows!
   (As He knows I'll do it again),
That smell of wattle round Lichtenberg,
   Riding in, in the rain!

I saw Sydney the same as ever,
   The picnics and brass-bands;
And the little homestead on Hunter River
   And my new vines joining hands.
It all came over me in one act
   Quick as a shot through the brain—
With the smell of the wattle round Lichtenberg,
   Riding in, in the rain!

I have forgotten a hundred fights,
   But one I shall not forget—
With the raindrops bunging up my sights
   And my eyes bunged up with wet;
And through the crack and the stink of the cordite
   (Ah Christ! My country again!)
The smell of the wattle by Lichtenberg,
   Riding in, in the rain!

STELLENBOSH

(COMPOSITE COLUMNS)

THE General 'eard the firin' on the flank
    An' 'e sent a mounted man to bring 'im back,
The silly, pushin' person's name an' rank,
    'Oo'd dared to answer Brother Boer's attack.
For there might 'ave been a serious engagement,
    An' 'e might 'ave wasted 'alf a dozen men;
So 'e ordered 'im to stop 'is operations round the
        kopjes,
    An' 'e told 'im off before the Staff at ten!

    An' it all goes into the laundry,
    But it never comes out in the wash,
    'Ow we're sugared about by the old men
    ('Eavy-sterned amateur old men!)
    That 'amper an' 'inder an' scold men
    For fear o' Stellenbosh!

183

STELLENBOSH

The General 'ad " produced a great effect,"
    The General 'ad the country cleared—almost;
The General "'ad no reason to expect,"
    And the Boers 'ad us bloomin' well on toast!
For we might 'ave crossed the drift before the
      twilight,
    Instead o' sittin' down an' takin' root;
But we was not allowed, so the Boojers scooped the
      crowd,
    To the last survivin' bandolier an' boot.

The General saw the farm'ouse in 'is rear,
    With its stoep so nicely shaded from the sun;
Sez 'e, " I'll pitch my tabernacle 'ere,"
    An' 'e kept us muckin' round till 'e 'ad done.
For 'e might 'ave caught the confluent pneumonia
    From sleepin' in his gaiters in the dew;
So 'e took a book an' dozed while the other columns
      closed
    And ——'s commando out an' trickled through!

The General saw the mountain-range ahead,
    With their 'elios showin' saucy on the 'eight,
So 'e 'eld us to the level ground instead,
    An' telegraphed the Boojers wouldn't fight.

184

For 'e might 'ave gone an' sprayed 'em with a
    pompom,
  Or 'e might 'ave slung a squadron out to see—
But 'e wasn't takin' chances in them 'igh an' 'ostile
    kranzes—
  He was markin' time to earn a K.C.B.

The General got 'is decorations thick
  (The men that backed 'is lies could not complain),
The Staff 'ad D.S.O.'s till we was sick,
  An' the soldier—'ad the work to do again!
For 'e might 'ave known the District was a 'otbed,
  Instead of 'andin' over, upside-down,
To a man 'oo 'ad to fight 'alf a year to put it right,
  While the General went an' slandered 'im in town!

    An' it all went into the laundry,
    But it never came out in the wash.
    We were sugared about by the old men
    (Panicky, perishin' old men)
    That 'amper an' 'inder an' scold men
    For fear o' Stellenbosh!

HALF-BALLAD OF WATERVAL

WHEN by the labour of my 'ands
  I've 'elped to pack a transport tight
With prisoners for foreign lands,
  I ain't transported with delight.
  I know it's only just an' right,
    But yet it somehow sickens me,
For I 'ave learned at Waterval
    The meanin' of captivity.

Be'ind the pegged barb-wire strands,
  Beneath the tall electric light,
We used to walk in bare-'ead bands,
  Explainin' 'ow we lost our fight.
  An' that is what they'll do to-night
    Upon the steamer out at sea,
If I 'ave learned at Waterval
    The meanin' of captivity.

186

HALF-BALLAD OF WATERVAL

They'll never know the shame that brands—
  Black shame no livin' down makes white,
The mockin' from the sentry-stands,
  The women's laugh, the gaoler's spite.
  We are too bloomin' much polite,
    But that is 'ow I'd 'ave us be . . .
Since I 'ave learned at Waterval
  The meanin' of captivity.

They'll get those draggin' days all right,
  Spent as a foreigner commands,
An' 'orrors of the locked-up night,
  With 'Ell's own thinkin' on their 'ands.
  I'd give the gold o' twenty Rands
    (If it was mine) to set 'em free . . .
For I 'ave learned at Waterval
  The meanin' of captivity!

PIET

(REGULAR OF THE LINE)

I DO not love my Empire's foes,
  Nor call 'em angels; still,
What *is* the sense of 'atin' those
  'Oom you are paid to kill?
So, barrin' all that foreign lot
  Which only joined for spite,
Myself, I'd just as soon as not
  Respect the man I fight.
    Ah there, Piet!—'is trousies to 'is knees,
    'Is coat-tails lyin' level in the bullet-
      sprinkled breeze;
    'E does not lose 'is rifle an' 'e does not lose
      'is seat,
    I've known a lot o' people ride a dam' sight
      worse than Piet!

PIET

I've 'eard 'im cryin' from the ground
  Like Abel's blood of old,
An' skirmished out to look, an' found
  The beggar nearly cold;
I've waited on till 'e was dead
  (Which couldn't 'elp 'im much),
But many grateful things 'e's said
  To me for doin' such.
    Ah there, Piet! whose time 'as come to die,
    'Is carcase past rebellion, but 'is eyes
      inquirin' why.
    Though dressed in stolen uniform with
      badge o' rank complete,
    I've known a lot o' fellers go a dam'
      sight worse than Piet.

An' when there wasn't aught to do
  But camp and cattle-guards,
I've fought with 'im the 'ole day through
  At fifteen 'undred yards;
Long afternoons o' lyin' still,
  An' 'earin' as you lay
The bullets swish from 'ill to 'ill
  Like scythes among the 'ay.
    Ah there, Piet! —be'ind 'is stony kop,
    With 'is Boer bread an' biltong, an' 'is flask
    of awful Dop;

'Is Mauser for amusement an' 'is pony for
  retreat,
I've known a lot o' fellers shoot a dam' sight
  worse than Piet.

He's shoved 'is rifle 'neath my nose
  Before I'd time to think,
An' borrowed all my Sunday clo'es
  An' sent me 'ome in pink;
An' I 'ave crept (Lord, 'ow I've crept!)
  On 'ands an' knees I've gone,
And spoored and floored and caught and kept
  An' sent him to Ceylon!
    Ah there, Piet!—you've sold me many a
      pup,
    When week on week alternate it was you
      an' me "'ands up!"
    But though I never made *you* walk man-
      naked in the 'eat,
    I've known a lot of fellers stalk a dam' sight
      worse than Piet.

From Plewman's to Marabastad,
  From Ookiep to De Aar,
Me an' my trusty friend 'ave 'ad,
  As you might say, a war;

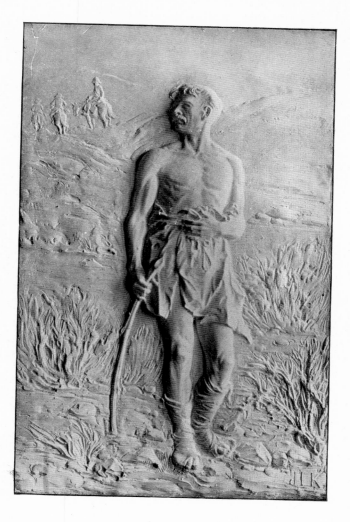

PIET

I ain't more proud of 'avin' won,
    Than I am pleased with Piet.
        Ah there, Piet!—picked up be'ind the
           drive!
        The wonder wasn't 'ow 'e fought, but 'ow
           'e kep' alive,
        With nothin' in 'is belly, on 'is back, or to
           'is feet—
        I've known a lot o' men behave a dam'
           sight worse than Piet.

No more I'll 'ear 'is rifle crack
    Along the block'ouse fence—
The beggar's on the peaceful tack,
    Regardless of expense.
For countin' what 'e eats an' draws,
    An' gifts an' loans as well,
'E's gettin' 'alf the Earth, because
    'E didn't give us 'Ell!
        Ah there, Piet! with your brand-new
           English plough,
        Your gratis tents an' cattle, an' your most
           ungrateful frow.
        You've made the British taxpayer rebuild
           your country-seat—
        I've known some pet battalions charge a
           dam' sight less than Piet.

"WILFUL-MISSING"

THERE is a world outside the one you know,
   To which for curiousness 'Ell can't compare—
It is the place where "wilful-missings" go,
   As we can testify, for we are there.

You may 'ave read a bullet laid us low,
   That we was gathered in "with reverent care"
And buried proper. But it was not so,
   As we can testify, for we are there.

They can't be certain—faces alter so
   After the old aasvogel's 'ad 'is share;
The uniform's the mark by which they go—
   And—ain't it odd?—the one we best can spare.

We might 'ave seen our chance to cut the show—
   Name, number, record, an' begin elsewhere—
Leavin' some not too late-lamented foe
   One funeral—private—British—for 'is share.

"WILFUL-MISSING"

We may 'ave took it yonder in the Low
   Bush-veldt that sends men stragglin' unaware
Among the Kaffirs, till their columns go,
   An' they are left past call or count or care.

We might 'ave been your lovers long ago,
   'Usbands or children — comfort or despair.
Our death (an' burial) settles all we owe,
   An' why we done it is our own affair.

Marry again, and we will not say no,
   Nor come to bastardize the kids you bear:
Wait on in 'ope — you've all your life below
   Before you'll ever 'ear us on the stair.

There is no need to give our reasons, though
   Gawd knows we all 'ad reasons which were fair;
But other people might not judge 'em so,
   And now it doesn't matter what they were.

What man can size or weigh another's woe?
   There are some things too bitter 'ard to bear.
Suffice it we 'ave finished — Domino!
   As we can testify, for we are there,
In the side-world where " wilful-missings " go.

UBIQUE

THERE is a word you often see, pronounce it as you
    may—
" You bike," " you bykwe," " ubbikwe "—alludin' to
    R. A.
It serves 'Orse, Field, an' Garrison as motto for a
    crest,
An' when you've found out all it means I'll tell you
    'alf the rest.

Ubique means the long-range Krupp be'ind the low-
    range 'ill—
Ubique means you'll pick it up an' while you do
    stand still.
Ubique means you've caught the flash an' timed it
    by the sound.
Ubique means five gunners' 'ash before you've loosed
    a round.

UBIQUE

Ubique means Blue Fuse, an' make the 'ole to sink
    the trail.
Ubique means stand up an' take the Mauser's 'alf-
    mile 'ail.
Ubique means the crazy team not God nor man can
    'old.
Ubique means that 'orse's scream which turns your
    innards cold!

Ubique means " Bank, 'Olborn, Bank—a penny all
    the way "—
The soothin', jingle-bump-an'-clank from day to
    peaceful day.
Ubique means "They've caught De Wet, an' now
    we shan't be long."
Ubique means " I much regret, the beggar's goin'
    strong!"

Ubique means the tearin' drift where, breech-blocks
    jammed with mud,
The khaki muzzles duck an' lift across the khaki
    flood.
Ubique means the dancin' plain that changes rocks
    to Boers.
Ubique means mirage again an' shellin' all
    outdoors.

UBIQUE

Ubique means " Entrain at once for Grootdefeat-
    fontein "!
Ubique means " Off-load your guns "—at midnight
    in the rain!
Ubique means " More mounted men.　Return all
    guns to store."
Ubique means the R. A. M. R. Infantillery Corps!

Ubique means that warnin' grunt the perished
    linesman knows,
When o'er 'is strung an' sufferin' front the shrapnel
    sprays 'is foes;
An' as their firin' dies away the 'usky whisper runs
From lips that 'aven't drunk all day : " The Guns!
    Thank Gawd, the Guns!"

Extreme, depressed, point-blank or short, end-first
    or any 'ow,
From Colesberg Kop to Quagga's Poort—from
    Ninety-Nine till now—
By what I've 'eard the others tell an' I in spots 'ave
    seen,
There's nothin' this side 'Eaven or 'Ell Ubique
    doesn't mean!

THE RETURN

(ALL ARMS)

PEACE is declared, an' I return
    To 'Ackneystadt, but not the same;
Things 'ave transpired which made me learn
    The size and meanin' of the game.
I did no more than others did,
    I don't know where the change began;
I started as a average kid,
    I finished as a thinkin' man.

If England was what England seems
    An' not the England of our dreams,
But only putty, brass, an' paint,
    'Ow quick we'd drop 'er! But she
    ain't !

THE RETURN

Before my gappin' mouth could speak
   I 'eard it in my comrade's tone;
I saw it on my neighbour's cheek
   Before I felt it flush my own.
An' last it come to me—not pride,
   Nor yet conceit, but on the 'ole
(If such a term may be applied),
   The makin's of a bloomin' soul.

Rivers at night that cluck an' jeer,
   Plains which the moonshine turns to sea,
Mountains that never let you near,
   An' stars to all eternity;
An' the quick-breathin' dark that fills
   The 'ollows of the wilderness,
When the wind worries through the 'ills—
   These may 'ave taught me more or less.

Towns without people, ten times took,
   An' ten times left an' burned at last;
An' starvin' dogs that come to look
   For owners when a column passed;
An' quiet, 'omesick talks between
   Men, met by night, you never knew
Until—'is face—by shellfire seen—
   Once—an' struck off. They taught me too.

THE RETURN

The day's lay-out—the mornin' sun
   Beneath your 'at-brim as you sight;
The dinner-'ush from noon till one,
   An' the full roar that lasts till night;
An' the pore dead that look so old
   An' was so young an hour ago,
An' legs tied down before they're cold—
   These are the things which make you know.

Also Time runnin' into years—
   A thousand Places left be'ind—
An' Men from both two 'emispheres
   Discussin' things of every kind;
So much more near than I 'ad known,
   So much more great than I 'ad guessed—
An' me, like all the rest, alone—
   But reachin' out to all the rest!

So 'ath it come to me—not pride,
   Nor yet conceit, but on the 'ole
(If such a term may be applied),
   The makin's of a bloomin' soul.
But now, discharged, I fall away
   To do with little things again. . . .
Gawd, 'oo knows all I cannot say,
   Look after me in Thamesfontein!

RECESSIONAL

Lo, all our pomp of yesterday
   Is one with Nineveh and Tyre!
Judge of the Nations, spare us yet,
Lest we forget—lest we forget!

If, drunk with sight of power, we loose
   Wild tongues that have not Thee in awe,
Such boastings as the Gentiles use,
   Or lesser breeds without the Law—
Lord God of Hosts, be with us yet,
Lest we forget—lest we forget!

For heathen heart that puts her trust
   In reeking tube and iron shard,
All valiant dust that builds on dust,
   And guarding, calls not Thee to guard,
For frantic boast and foolish word—
Thy Mercy on Thy People, Lord!

                           Amen.